perfect
salads

Bath · New York · Singapore · Hong Kong · Cologne · Delhi · Melbourne

This edition published by Parragon in 2009

Parragon Publishing
Queen Street House
4 Queen Street
Bath BA1 1HE, UK

ISBN 978-1-4075-4829-6

Printed in China

This book uses imperial, metric, and U.S. cup measurements. Follow the same units of measurement throughout; do not mix imperial and metric. All spoon measurements are level, unless otherwise stated: teaspoons are assumed to be 5ml, and tablespoons are assumed to be 15ml. Unless otherwise stated, milk is assumed to be whole, eggs and individual fruit, such as bananas, are medium, and pepper is freshly ground black pepper.

Recipes using raw or very lightly cooked eggs should be avoided by infants, the elderly, pregnant women, convalescents, and anyone with a chronic condition. Pregnant and breastfeeding women are advised to avoid eating peanuts and peanut products.

perfect
salads

introduction

Whether served as a summery main course, a refreshing side dish, an intriguing warm appetizer, an easy to transport picnic dish, or a quick lunch, salads are wonderfully versatile. Ingredients ranging from meat, poultry, fish, cheese, and eggs to vegetables, beans, fruit, seeds, pasta, and grains can be mixed and matched into endless delicious combinations. Dressings may be equally diverse—a squeeze of lemon and a drizzle of oil or a classic herb vinaigrette, creamy mayonnaise or a low-fat yogurt sauce, a combination of subtle Asian herbs and spices or a mind-blowing Caribbean concoction of tropical fruit juice and chiles.

Successful salads depend on using the best-quality

ingredients. Limp greens, overripe tomatoes, dried-up cheese, and soggy pasta will not be improved by mixing them together or disguised by smothering them with dressing. Traditional salad ingredients, such as lettuce, cucumber, and celery, must be really fresh. Fruit, whether

mangoes and strawberries or those that are considered vegetables, such as tomatoes and bell peppers, should be ripe and bursting with flavor. Keep an eye on the expiration dates of pantry ingredients—nuts, seeds, and oils quickly become rancid and ground spices soon lose their flavor. Finally, as a general rule, don't add the dressing to a salad until you are ready to serve it.

We are driven crazy these days with advice to eat more healthily and to include more fruit and vegetables in our diet. Salads make this easy because a mixture of different colored fruit and vegetables—a typical salad—is guaranteed to provide a wide range of nutrients and plenty of fiber. Many ingredients are used raw, thus conserving their vitamin content. Monounsaturated oils,

such as olive and canola, can help protect against high blood cholesterol, while the addition of seeds supplies essential omega-6. Finally, as flavorings for dressings—garlic, herbs, mustard, fruit juice, wine vinegars, nut oils—are so tasty, you'll find it easy to cut down your salt intake. Super foods with super flavor—on a plate.

classic salads

Many classic salads were first put together by family cooks mixing and matching the finest and freshest local ingredients into a harmonious combination, and these quickly became regional specialties. Almost every country has its own favorite. What Italian could resist the partnership of melon and prosciutto, and would a Greek consider a meal complete without a salad featuring juicy black olives, sun-ripened tomatoes, and piquant feta cheese?

At the other end of the scale, recipes were specially created by world-famous professional chefs, many of whose own names or the names of their establishments became synonymous with their classic salads. Caesar Cardini lives on in his inspired, yet simple mixture of crisp greens, crusty croutons, and tangy Parmesan tossed in a rich, anchovy-flavored dressing. Serve diced apple, celery, and walnuts in a light mayonnaise and you evoke the glamorous style of New York's celebrated Waldorf Astoria hotel.

Classic salads may be simple or luxurious, economical or extravagant. Some are served as a main course, while others make a perfect side dish. They feature ingredients as diverse as beans, pasta, chicken, and lobster, but whether they started life in a grand Parisian hotel or an obscure Italian farmhouse, they have stood the test of time and truly become classics.

salad niçoise

ingredients

SERVES 4

2 tuna steaks, about
    3/4 inch/2 cm thick
olive oil, for brushing
9 oz/250 g green beans,
    trimmed
1/2 cup vinaigrette or garlic
    vinaigrette dressing
2 hearts of lettuce, leaves
    separated
3 large hard-cooked eggs,
    cut into quarters
2 juicy vine-ripened tomatoes,
    cut into wedges
1 3/4 oz/50 g anchovy fillets in
    oil, drained
2 oz/55 g Niçoise olives, pitted
salt and pepper

method

1 Heat a ridged, cast-iron grill pan over high heat until you can feel the heat rising from the surface. Brush the tuna steaks with oil, place oiled-side down on the hot pan, and cook for 2 minutes. Lightly brush the top sides of the tuna steaks with more oil. Use a pair of tongs to turn the tuna steaks over, then season to taste with salt and pepper. Continue cooking for another 2 minutes for rare or up to 4 minutes for well done. Let cool.

2 Meanwhile, bring a pan of salted water to a boil. Add the beans to the pan and return to a boil, then boil for 3 minutes, or until tender-crisp. Drain the beans and immediately transfer them to a large bowl. Pour over the vinaigrette and stir together, then let the beans cool in the dressing.

3 To serve, line a platter with lettuce leaves. Lift the beans out of the bowl, leaving the excess dressing behind, and pile them in the center of the platter. Break the tuna into large pieces and arrange it over the beans. Arrange the hard-cooked eggs and the tomatoes around the side. Arrange the anchovy fillets over the salad, then scatter with the olives. Drizzle the remaining dressing over the salad and serve.

chicken, cheese & arugula salad

ingredients

SERVES 4

5^1/$_2$ oz/150 g arugula leaves

2 celery stalks, trimmed and
  sliced

^{1}/$_2$ cucumber, sliced

2 scallions, trimmed and
  sliced

2 tbsp chopped fresh parsley

^{1}/$_4$ cup walnut pieces

12 oz/350 g boneless roast
  chicken, sliced

4^1/$_2$ oz/125 g bleu cheese,
  cubed

handful of seedless red grapes,
  cut in half (optional)

salt and pepper

dressing

2 tbsp olive oil

1 tbsp sherry vinegar

1 tsp Dijon mustard

1 tbsp chopped mixed herbs

method

1 Wash the arugula leaves, pat dry with paper towels, and put them into a large salad bowl. Add the celery, cucumber, scallions, parsley, and walnuts and mix together well. Transfer onto a large serving platter. Arrange the chicken slices over the salad, then scatter over the cheese. Add the red grapes, if using. Season well with salt and pepper.

2 To make the dressing, put all the ingredients into a screw-top jar and shake well. Alternatively, put them into a bowl and mix together well. Drizzle the dressing over the salad and serve.

greek feta salad

ingredients

SERVES 4

a few grape leaves

4 tomatoes, sliced

$^1/_2$ cucumber, peeled and
 sliced

1 small red onion, sliced
 thinly

4 oz/115 g feta cheese, cubed

8 black olives

dressing

3 tbsp extra virgin olive oil

1 tbsp lemon juice

$^1/_2$ tsp dried oregano

salt and pepper

method

1 To make the dressing, put the oil, lemon juice, oregano, and salt and pepper to taste in a screw-top jar and shake together until blended.

2 Arrange the grape leaves on a serving dish and then the tomatoes, cucumber, and onion. Sprinkle the cheese and olives on top. Pour the dressing over the salad and serve.

chef's salad

ingredients

SERVES 6

1 iceberg lettuce, shredded

6 oz/175 g cooked lean ham,
cut into thin strips

6 oz/175 g cooked tongue,
cut into thin strips

12 oz/350 g cooked chicken,
cut into thin strips

6 oz/175 g Gruyère cheese

4 tomatoes, quartered

3 hard-cooked eggs, shelled
and quartered

1 3/4 cups Thousand Island
Dressing

sliced French bread, to serve

method

1 Arrange the lettuce on a large serving platter.
Arrange the cold meats decoratively on top.

2 Cut the Gruyère cheese into thin cubes.

3 Arrange the cheese cubes over the salad,
and the tomato and egg quarters around the
edge of the platter. Serve the salad
immediately with the Thousand Island
Dressing and sliced French bread.

red onion, tomato & herb salad

ingredients

SERVES 4

2 lb/900 g tomatoes, thinly
    sliced
1 tbsp sugar (optional)
1 red onion, thinly sliced
large handful of coarsely
    chopped fresh herbs,
    using any in season,
    such as tarragon, sorrel,
    cilantro, or basil
salt and pepper

dressing

2–4 tbsp vegetable oil
2 tbsp red wine vinegar or
    fruit vinegar

method

1 Arrange the tomato slices in a shallow bowl. Sprinkle with sugar (if using), and salt and pepper to taste.

2 Separate the onion slices into rings and sprinkle them over the tomatoes. Sprinkle the chopped fresh herbs over the top.

3 Place the dressing ingredients in a jar with a screw-top lid. Shake well. Pour the dressing over the salad and mix gently.

4 Cover with plastic wrap and chill for 20 minutes. Remove the salad from the refrigerator 5 minutes before serving, unwrap the dish, and stir gently before setting out on the table.

caesar salad

ingredients

SERVES 4

$^2/_3$ cup olive oil

2 garlic cloves

5 slices white bread,
    crusts removed, cut into
    $^1/_2$-inch/1-cm cubes

1 large egg

2 romaine lettuce or
    3 Boston lettuce

2 tbsp lemon juice

8 canned anchovy fillets,
    drained and coarsely
    chopped

$^3/_4$ cup fresh Parmesan
    cheese shavings

salt and pepper

method

1 Bring a small, heavy-bottom pan of water to a boil.

2 Meanwhile, heat 4 tablespoons of the olive oil in a heavy-bottom skillet. Add the garlic and cubed bread and cook, stirring and tossing frequently, for 4–5 minutes, or until the bread is crispy and golden all over. Remove from the skillet with a slotted spoon and drain on paper towels.

3 Arrange the salad greens in a salad bowl. Mix the remaining olive oil and lemon juice together, then season to taste with salt and pepper. Crack the egg into the dressing and whisk to blend. Pour the dressing over the salad greens, toss well, then add the croutons and chopped anchovies and toss the salad again. Sprinkle with Parmesan cheese shavings and serve.

tuna & avocado salad

ingredients

SERVES 4

2 avocados, pitted, peeled,
  and cubed

9 oz/250 g cherry tomatoes,
  halved

2 red bell peppers, seeded
  and chopped

1 bunch fresh flat-leaf
  parsley, chopped

2 garlic cloves, crushed

1 fresh red chile, seeded and
  finely chopped

juice of $1/2$ lemon

6 tbsp olive oil

3 tbsp sesame seeds

4 fresh tuna steaks, about
  $5^1/2$ oz/150 g each

8 cooked new potatoes, cubed

pepper

arugula leaves and crusty
  bread, to serve

method

1 Toss the avocados, tomatoes, red bell peppers, parsley, garlic, chile, lemon juice, and 2 tablespoons of the oil together in a large bowl. Season to taste with pepper, cover, and let chill in the refrigerator for 30 minutes.

2 Lightly crush the sesame seeds in a mortar with a pestle. Tip the crushed seeds onto a plate and spread out. Press each tuna steak in turn into the crushed seeds to coat on both sides.

3 Heat 2 tablespoons of the remaining oil in a skillet, add the potatoes, and cook, stirring frequently, for 5–8 minutes, or until crisp and brown. Remove from the skillet and drain on paper towels.

4 Wipe out the skillet, add the remaining oil, and heat over high heat until very hot. Add the tuna steaks and cook for 3–4 minutes on each side.

5 To serve, divide the avocado salad among 4 serving plates. Top each with a tuna steak, sprinkle over the potatoes and arugula leaves, and serve with crusty bread.

tomato, mozzarella & avocado salad

ingredients

SERVES 4

2 ripe beefsteak tomatoes

5^1/$_2$ oz/150 g fresh mozzarella

2 avocados

4 tbsp olive oil

1^1/$_2$ tbsp white wine vinegar

1 tsp coarse-grain mustard

few fresh basil leaves,
    torn into pieces

20 black olives

salt and pepper

method

1 Using a sharp knife, cut the tomatoes into thick wedges and place in a large serving dish. Drain the mozzarella and coarsely tear into pieces. Cut the avocados in half and remove the pits and skin. Cut the flesh into slices, then arrange the mozzarella and avocado with the tomatoes.

2 Mix the oil, vinegar, and mustard together in a small bowl, add salt and pepper to taste, then drizzle over the salad.

3 Sprinkle the basil and olives over the top and serve at once.

waldorf summer chicken salad

ingredients

SERVES 4

1 lb 2 oz/500 g red apples,
   diced
3 tbsp fresh lemon juice
$2/3$ cup light mayonnaise
1 head celery
4 shallots, sliced
1 garlic clove, finely chopped
$3/4$ cup walnuts, chopped
1 lb 2 oz/500 g cooked
   chicken, cubed
1 cos lettuce
pepper
chopped walnuts, to garnish

method

1 Place the apples in a bowl with the lemon juice and 1 tablespoon of the mayonnaise. Leave for 40 minutes.

2 Using a sharp knife, slice the celery very thinly. Add the celery, shallots, garlic, and walnuts to the apple and mix together. Stir in the remaining mayonnaise and blend thoroughly.

3 Add the cooked chicken to the bowl and mix well.

4 Line a serving dish with the lettuce and pile the chicken salad on top. Sprinkle with pepper and garnish with the chopped walnuts.

warm pasta salad

ingredients

SERVES 4

8 oz/225 g dried farfalle or
   other pasta shapes
6 pieces of sun-dried tomato
   in oil, drained and
   chopped
4 scallions, chopped
$1^1/_4$ cups arugula, shredded
$^1/_2$ cucumber, seeded and
   diced
salt and pepper

dressing

4 tbsp olive oil
1 tbsp white wine vinegar
$^1/_2$ tsp superfine sugar
1 tsp Dijon mustard
4 fresh basil leaves, finely
   shredded
salt and pepper

method

1 To make the dressing, whisk the olive oil, vinegar, sugar, and mustard together in a bowl or pitcher. Season to taste with salt and pepper and stir in the basil.

2 Bring a large, heavy-bottom pan of lightly salted water to a boil. Add the pasta, return to a boil, and cook for 8–10 minutes, or until tender but still firm to the bite. Drain and transfer to a salad bowl. Add the dressing and toss well.

3 Add the tomatoes, scallions, arugula, and cucumber, season to taste with salt and pepper, and toss. Serve warm.

lobster salad

ingredients

SERVES 2

2 raw lobster tails

radicchio leaves

fresh dill sprigs, to garnish

lemon-dill mayonnaise

1 large lemon

1 large egg yolk

$1/2$ tsp Dijon mustard

$2/3$ cup olive oil

1 tbsp chopped fresh dill

salt and pepper

method

1 To make the lemon-dill mayonnaise, finely grate half the lemon rind and squeeze the juice. Beat the egg yolk in a small bowl, then beat in the mustard and 1 teaspoon of the lemon juice.

2 Using a balloon whisk or electric mixer, beat the oil into the egg yolk mixture, drop by drop, until a thick mayonnaise forms. Stir in the lemon rind and 1 tablespoon of the remaining lemon juice.

3 Season the mayonnaise to taste with salt and pepper and add more lemon juice if desired. Stir in the dill, cover, and let chill in the refrigerator until required.

4 Bring a large pan of lightly salted water to a boil. Add the lobster tails, return to a boil, and cook for 6 minutes, or until the flesh is opaque and the shells are red. Drain at once and set aside to cool.

5 Remove the lobster flesh from the shells and cut into bite-size pieces. Arrange the radicchio leaves on individual plates and top with the lobster flesh. Place a spoonful of the lemon-dill mayonnaise on the side. Garnish with dill sprigs and serve.

salad of greens with lemon dressing

ingredients

SERVES 4

7 oz/200 g mixed baby salad
   leaves, such as maché,
   spinach, watercress, and
   wild arugula
4 tbsp mixed chopped fresh
   herbs, such as flat-leaf
   parsley, mint, cilantro,
   and basil

dressing

4 tbsp extra virgin olive oil
juice of about $1/2$ lemon
1 garlic clove, crushed
salt and pepper

method

1 Wash the salad leaves and discard any thick stems. Dry and put in a salad bowl. Add the chopped herbs.

2 To make the dressing whisk together the oil, lemon juice, garlic, and salt and pepper to taste in a small bowl. Taste and add more oil or lemon juice if necessary.

3 Just before serving, whisk the dressing; pour over the salad leaves, toss, and serve.

pasta salad with charbroiled bell peppers

ingredients

SERVES 4

1 red bell pepper

1 orange bell pepper

10 oz/280 g dried conchiglie

5 tbsp extra virgin olive oil

2 tbsp lemon juice

2 tbsp green pesto

1 garlic clove, finely chopped

3 tbsp shredded fresh basil
   leaves

salt and pepper

method

1 Preheat the broiler. Put the whole bell peppers on a baking sheet and place under the hot broiler, turning frequently, for 15 minutes, or until charred all over. Remove with tongs and place in a bowl. Cover with crumpled paper towels and reserve.

2 Meanwhile, bring a large saucepan of lightly salted water to a boil. Add the pasta, return to a boil, and cook for 8–10 minutes, or until tender but still firm to the bite.

3 Combine the olive oil, lemon juice, pesto, and garlic in a bowl, whisking well to mix. Drain the pasta, add it to the pesto mixture while still hot, and toss well. Reserve until required.

4 When the bell peppers are cool enough to handle, peel off the skins, then cut open and remove the seeds. Chop the flesh coarsely and add to the pasta with the basil. Season to taste with salt and pepper and toss well. Serve.

prosciutto with melon & asparagus

ingredients

SERVES 4

8 oz/225 g asparagus spears
1 small or $^1/_2$ medium-size
    galia or cantaloupe melon
2 oz/55 g prosciutto, thinly
    sliced
5$^1/_2$ oz/150 g bag mixed salad
    greens, such as herb
    salad with arugula
$^5/_8$ cup fresh raspberries
1 tbsp freshly shaved
    Parmesan cheese

dressing

1 tbsp balsamic vinegar
2 tbsp raspberry vinegar
2 tbsp orange juice

method

1 Trim the asparagus, cutting in half if very long. Cook in lightly salted boiling water over medium heat for 5 minutes, or until tender. Drain and plunge into cold water, then drain again and set aside.

2 Cut the melon in half and scoop out the seeds. Cut into small wedges and cut away the rind. Separate the prosciutto slices, cut in half, and wrap around the melon wedges.

3 Arrange the salad greens on a large serving platter and place the melon wedges on top together with the asparagus spears.

4 Scatter over the raspberries and Parmesan shavings.

5 Place the vinegars and juice in a screw-top jar and shake until blended. Pour over the salad and serve.

mushroom salad

ingredients

SERVES 4

8 oz/225 g white or pink
 cremini mushrooms,
 thinly sliced

finely grated rind and juice of
 1/2 lemon

3 tbsp sour cream

1 tbsp chopped fresh chervil

salt and pepper

method

1 Put the mushrooms in a large bowl, sprinkle with the lemon rind and juice, and toss well. Gently stir in the sour cream and season with salt and pepper.

2 Cover the bowl with plastic wrap and let stand, stirring once or twice, for 1 hour. Spoon the salad into a serving bowl, sprinkle with the chervil, and serve.

italian salad

ingredients

SERVES 4

8 oz/225 g dried conchiglie
1³/₄ oz/50 g pine nuts
12 oz/350 g cherry tomatoes,
    cut in half
1 red bell pepper, seeded and
    cut into bite-size chunks
1 red onion, chopped
7 oz/200 g buffalo mozzarella,
    cubed
12 black olives, pitted
1 oz/25 g fresh basil leaves
shavings of fresh Parmesan
    cheese, to garnish
crusty bread, to serve

dressing

5 tbsp extra virgin olive oil
2 tbsp balsamic vinegar
1 tbsp chopped fresh basil
salt and pepper

method

1 Bring a large pan of lightly salted water to a boil. Add the pasta and cook over medium heat for about 10 minutes, or according to the package instructions. When cooked, the pasta should be tender but still firm to the bite. Drain, rinse under cold running water, and drain again. Let cool.

2 While the pasta is cooking, put the pine nuts in a dry skillet and cook over low heat for 1–2 minutes, until golden brown. Remove from the heat, transfer to a dish, and let cool.

3 To make the dressing, put the oil, vinegar, and basil into a small bowl. Season with salt and pepper and stir together well. Cover with plastic wrap and set to one side.

4 To assemble the salad, divide the pasta between serving bowls. Add the pine nuts, tomatoes, red bell pepper, onion, cheese, and olives. Scatter over the basil leaves, then drizzle over the dressing. Garnish with fresh Parmesan cheese shavings and serve with crusty bread.

smoked chicken salad with avocado & tarragon dressing

ingredients

SERVES 4–6

2 large tomatoes, sliced

1 lb 5 oz/600 g smoked chicken, skinned and cut into slices

9 oz/250 g fresh watercress, any thick stems or yellow leaves removed, then rinsed and patted dry

3 oz/75 g fresh bean sprouts, soaked for 20 minutes in cold water, then drained well and patted dry

leaves from several sprigs fresh flat-leaf parsley or cilantro

dressing

1 ripe, soft avocado

2 tbsp lemon juice

1 tbsp tarragon vinegar

3 oz/75 g thick plain yogurt

1 small garlic clove, crushed

1 tbsp chopped fresh tarragon leaves

salt and pepper

method

1 To make the dressing, put the avocado, lemon juice, and vinegar in a blender or food processor and blend until smooth, scraping down the side with a rubber spatula. Add the yogurt, garlic, and tarragon leaves and process again. Season with salt and pepper to taste, then transfer to a bowl. Cover closely with plastic wrap and chill for 2 hours.

2 To assemble the salad, divide the tomato slices among 4–6 individual plates. Toss the smoked chicken, watercress, bean sprouts, and parsley or cilantro leaves together. Divide the salad ingredients among the plates.

3 Adjust the seasoning in the dressing, if necessary. Spoon the dressing over each salad and serve.

potato salad

ingredients

SERVES 4

1 lb 9 oz/700 g new potatoes
8 scallions
1 cup mayonnaise
1 tsp paprika, plus extra
   pinch to garnish
salt and pepper
2 tbsp snipped fresh chives

method

1 Bring a large pan of lightly salted water to a boil. Add the potatoes and cook for 10–15 minutes, or until just tender.

2 Drain the potatoes and rinse them under cold running water until completely cold. Drain again. Transfer the potatoes to a bowl and reserve until required.

3 Using a sharp knife, slice the scallions thinly on the diagonal.

4 Mix the mayonnaise, paprika, and salt and pepper to taste together in a bowl. Pour the mixture over the potatoes. Add the scallions to the potatoes and toss together.

5 Transfer the potato salad to a serving bowl and sprinkle with snipped chives and a pinch of paprika. Cover and let chill in the refrigerator until required.

warm goat cheese salad

ingredients

SERVES 4

1 small iceberg lettuce,
　torn into pieces
handful of arugula leaves
few radicchio leaves, torn
6 slices French bread
4 oz/115 g goat cheese, sliced

dressing

4 tbsp extra virgin olive oil
1 tbsp white wine vinegar
salt and pepper

method

1 Preheat the broiler. Divide all the leaves among 4 individual salad bowls.

2 Toast one side of the bread under the broiler until golden. Place a slice of cheese on top of each untoasted side and toast until the cheese is just melting.

3 Put all the dressing ingredients into a bowl and beat together until combined. Pour over the leaves, tossing to coat.

4 Cut each slice of bread in half and place 3 halves on top of each salad. Toss very gently to combine and serve warm.

russian salad

ingredients

4 oz/115 g new potatoes

generous 1 cup frozen or
    shelled fresh fava beans

4 oz/115 g baby carrots

4 oz/115 g baby corn

4 oz/115 g baby turnips

4 oz/115 g white mushrooms,
    cut into thin sticks

12 oz/350 g cooked, shelled
    shrimp, deveined

$1/2$ cup mayonnaise

1 tbsp lemon juice

2 tbsp bottled capers, drained
    and rinsed

2 tbsp extra virgin olive oil

2 hard-cooked eggs, shelled
    and halved

4 canned anchovy fillets,
    drained and halved

salt and pepper

paprika, to garnish

method

1 Cook the new potatoes, fava beans, carrots, corn, and turnips simultaneously. Cook the potatoes in a large, heavy-bottom pan of lightly salted boiling water for 20 minutes. Cook the fava beans in a small pan of lightly salted water for 3 minutes, then drain, refresh under cold running water, and set aside until required. Cook the carrots, corn, and turnips in a large, heavy-bottom pan of lightly salted boiling water for 6 minutes.

2 Mix the mushrooms and shrimp together in a bowl. Mix the mayonnaise and lemon juice together in a separate bowl, then fold half the mixture into the shrimp mixture. Fold in the capers and season to taste with salt and pepper.

3 Drain the mixed vegetables, refresh under cold running water, and tip into a bowl. When the potatoes are cooked, drain, refresh under cold running water, and tip into the bowl. Pop the fava beans out of their skins by pinching them between your index finger and thumb and add to the bowl. Add the olive oil and toss to coat. Divide the potatoes and vegetables between serving plates and top with the shrimp mixture. Place a hard-cooked egg half in the center of each and garnish with the halved anchovies. Dust the eggs with paprika and serve with the remaining mayonnaise mixture.

asparagus & tomato salad

ingredients

SERVES 4

8 oz/225 g asparagus spears

1 lamb's lettuce, washed and
torn

1 handful arugula or mizuna
leaves

1 lb/450 g ripe tomatoes,
sliced

12 black olives, pitted and
sliced

1 tbsp toasted pine nuts

dressing

1 tsp lemon oil

1 tbsp olive oil

1 tsp whole-grain mustard

2 tbsp balsamic vinegar

salt and pepper

method

1 Steam the asparagus spears for 8 minutes, or until tender. Rinse under cold running water to prevent them from cooking any further, then cut into 2-inch/5-cm pieces.

2 Arrange the lettuce and arugula or mizuna leaves around a salad platter to form the base of the salad. Place the sliced tomatoes in a circle on top and the asparagus in the center. Sprinkle the black olives and pine nuts over the top.

3 To make the dressing, put the lemon oil, olive oil, mustard, and vinegar in a screw-top jar and season to taste with salt and black pepper. Shake vigorously and drizzle over the salad.

smoked salmon & wild arugula salad

ingredients

SERVES 4

1³/₄ oz/50 g wild arugula
   leaves
1 tbsp chopped fresh flat-leaf
   parsley
2 scallions, finely diced
2 large avocados
1 tbsp lemon juice
9 oz/250 g smoked salmon

dressing

²/₃ cup mayonnaise
2 tbsp lime juice
finely grated rind of 1 lime
1 tbsp chopped fresh flat-leaf
   parsley, plus extra sprigs
   to garnish

method

1 Shred the arugula and arrange in 4 individual glass bowls. Sprinkle over the chopped parsley and scallions.

2 Halve, peel, and pit the avocados and cut into thin slices or small chunks. Brush with the lemon juice to prevent discoloration, then divide among the salad bowls. Mix together gently. Cut the smoked salmon into strips and sprinkle over the top.

3 To make the dressing, put the mayonnaise in a bowl, then add the lemon juice, lime rind, and chopped parsley. Mix together well. Spoon some of the mayonnaise dressing on top of each salad and garnish with parsley sprigs.

avocado salad

ingredients

large handful of radicchio

large handful of arugula

1 small galia melon

2 ripe avocados

1 tbsp lemon juice

7 oz/200 g fontina cheese,
    cut into bite-size pieces

dressing

5 tbsp lemon-flavored or extra
    virgin olive oil

1 tbsp white wine vinegar

1 tbsp lemon juice

1 tbsp chopped fresh parsley

method

1 To make the dressing, mix together the oil, vinegar, lemon juice, and parsley in a small bowl.

2 Arrange the radicchio and arugula on serving plates. Cut the melon in half, then seed it and cut the flesh away from the skin. Discard the skin. Slice the melon flesh and arrange it over the salad greens.

3 Cut the avocados in half and remove and discard the pits and skin. Slice the flesh and brush with lemon juice. Arrange the slices over the melon, then scatter over the cheese. Drizzle over the dressing and serve.

three-bean salad

ingredients

SERVES 4–6

6 oz/175 g mixed salad
   greens, such as spinach,
   arugula, and frisée
1 red onion
3 oz/85 g radishes
6 oz/175 g cherry tomatoes
4 oz/115 g cooked beet
10 oz/280 g canned
   cannellini beans, drained
   and rinsed
7 oz/200 g canned red kidney
   beans, drained and rinsed
10$^{1}/_{2}$ oz/300 g canned
   flageolets, drained and
   rinsed
scant $^{1}/_{3}$ cup dried
   cranberries
scant $^{1}/_{2}$ cup roasted cashew
   nuts
8 oz/225 g feta cheese
   (drained weight), crumbled

dressing

4 tbsp extra virgin olive oil
1 tsp Dijon mustard
2 tbsp lemon juice
1 tbsp chopped fresh cilantro
salt and pepper

method

1 Arrange the salad greens in a salad bowl and set aside.

2 Cut the onion in half and thinly slice to form semicircles. Put into a bowl.

3 Thinly slice the radishes, cut the tomatoes in half, and peel the beet, if necessary, and dice. Add to the onion with the remaining ingredients, except the nuts and cheese.

4 To make the dressing, put all the ingredients into a screw-top jar and shake until blended. Pour over the bean mixture, toss lightly, then spoon on top of the salad greens.

5 Sprinkle over the nuts and cheese and serve at once.

fruit & vegetable salads

For many people, the word salad conjures up a picture of mixed raw vegetables and greens, perhaps with the addition of olives, beet, or even fresh herbs, and certainly this is a tasty and healthy combination, but it may seem less than exciting. In fact, vegetable salads are among the most varied and imaginative.

The range of suitable ingredients is vast—from lentils to cauliflower and from bell peppers to bean sprouts—and they can be combined in an almost endless variety of ways, especially if you include fruit, nuts, cheese, or eggs too. Salad vegetables don't all have to be raw. Some are best blanched or wilted and then cooled before the salad is assembled, while others benefit from more thorough cooking. Warm salads, where all or some of the ingredients retain some of the heat from being cooked, make especially good appetizers.

Besides excellent first courses, there are recipes for delicious side dishes and great main course salads for family lunches and informal entertaining. You may even be encouraged to mix and match different dishes for a simple but tempting buffet table. With inspiration for salads from countries as far apart as Greece and Vietnam, you will find an almost limitless source of clever ideas that make vegetable salads an irresistible treat.

green bean salad with feta

ingredients

SERVES 4

12 oz/350 g green beans, trimmed

1 red onion, chopped

3–4 tbsp chopped fresh cilantro

2 radishes, thinly sliced

3/4 cup crumbled feta cheese

1 tsp chopped fresh oregano or 1/2 tsp dried oregano

2 tbsp red wine vinegar or fruit vinegar

5 tbsp extra virgin olive oil

3 ripe tomatoes (optional), cut into wedges

pepper

method

1 Bring about 2 inches/5 cm water to a boil in the bottom of a steamer or in a medium saucepan. Add the green beans to the top of the steamer or place them in a metal colander set over the saucepan of water. Cover and steam the beans for about 5 minutes, until just tender.

2 Transfer the beans to a bowl and add the onion, cilantro, radishes, crumbled feta cheese, and oregano.

3 Grind pepper over to taste. Whisk the vinegar and olive oil together and then pour over the salad. Toss gently to mix well.

4 Transfer to a serving platter, surround with the tomato wedges if using, and serve at once or chill until ready to serve.

feta, mint & strawberry salad with green beans & pistachios

ingredients

SERVES 4–6

1 lb 2 oz/500 g fine green
   beans
1 lb 2 oz/500 g strawberries
2–3 tbsp pistachios
1 small bunch fresh mint
   leaves
1 lb 2 oz/500 g feta cheese
   (drained weight)
salt and pepper

dressing

2 tbsp raspberry vinegar
2 tsp superfine sugar
1 tbsp Dijon mustard
pinch of salt
$1/2$ cup olive oil

method

1 To make the dressing, mix the vinegar, sugar, mustard, and salt together in a bowl until smooth. Slowly pour in the oil, whisking constantly until the mixture has emulsified. Cover and refrigerate until required.

2 Blanch the beans in a large saucepan of salted boiling water for 1–2 minutes, so that they retain plenty of crunch. Drain and quickly toss in a large, cool bowl. Hull and halve the strawberries, then add to the beans. Stir in the pistachios and mint leaves. Toss the salad with enough of the dressing to coat lightly.

3 Break the feta cheese into chunks and scatter over the salad. Add a good grinding of pepper and serve immediately.

herbed mixed bean salad with fried provolone cheese

ingredients

SERVES 4–6

4 oz/115 g green beans, trimmed and cut into bite-size pieces

4 oz/115 g shelled fava beans, gray outer skins removed if not young

4 oz/115 g fresh or frozen shelled peas

14 oz/400 g canned cannellini or red kidney beans, drained and rinsed

1 small red onion, thinly sliced

2 tbsp chopped fresh parsley

1 tbsp snipped fresh chives

3 oz/85 g arugula or watercress leaves

dressing

5 tbsp extra virgin olive oil

2 tbsp tarragon vinegar

1/2 tsp mixed-grain mustard

pinch of sugar

salt and pepper

fried provolone cheese

olive oil

12 oz/350 g provolone cheese, cut into 12 slices

all-purpose flour, for dusting

method

1 Put the oil, vinegar, mustard, sugar, and salt and pepper to taste in a small screw-top jar and shake until blended and emulsified. Set aside.

2 Prepare a bowl of iced water. Bring a pan of lightly salted water to a boil. Add the green beans and fava beans and blanch for 3 minutes, or until just tender. Use a slotted spoon to remove the beans from the water and immediately transfer them to the iced water.

3 Return the water to a boil and blanch the peas for 3 minutes, or until tender. Remove from the water and add to the iced water to cool. Drain the beans and peas and pat dry with paper towels. Transfer to a large bowl, add the dressing, cannellini beans, onion, and herbs and toss. Cover and chill.

4 To make the Fried Provolone Cheese, heat the oil in a skillet over medium–high heat. Dust the cheese with flour, shaking off the excess, and add to the skillet. Fry for 3–6 minutes, or until golden. Flip the cheese over and cook the other side, then remove and keep warm while you fry the remaining pieces.

5 Divide the salad among individual plates, season, and add the cheese alongside. Drizzle the cheese with olive oil and serve.

green & white bean salad

ingredients

SERVES 4

$^1/_2$ cup dried Great Northern
  beans, soaked overnight
8 oz/225 g fine green beans,
  trimmed
$^1/_4$ red onion, thinly sliced
12 black olives, pitted
1 tbsp chopped chives
salt

dressing

$^1/_2$ tbsp lemon juice
$^1/_2$ tsp Dijon mustard
6 tbsp extra virgin olive oil
salt and pepper

method

1 Drain the soaked beans and put in a saucepan with plenty of fresh water to cover. Bring to a boil, then boil rapidly for 15 minutes. Reduce the heat slightly and cook for an additional 30 minutes, or until tender but not disintegrating. Add salt in the last 5 minutes of cooking. Drain and set aside.

2 Meanwhile, plunge the green beans into a large pan of boiling water. Return to a boil and cook for 4 minutes, until just tender but still brightly colored and crunchy. Drain and set aside.

3 Whisk together the dressing ingredients, then let stand.

4 While both types of bean are still slightly warm, tip them into a warmed shallow serving dish or arrange on warmed individual plates. Scatter over the onion slices, olives, and chives.

5 Whisk the dressing again and spoon over the salad. Serve immediately, at room temperature.

fava bean salad

ingredients

SERVES 4

5 lb 8 oz/2.5 kg young fava
  beans in their pods, shelled
  to give about 14 oz/400 g,
  or 15 oz/425 g frozen baby
  fava beans
2 tomatoes, peeled, seeded,
  and diced
3 tbsp shredded basil
1³/₄ oz/50 g Parmesan
  shavings

dressing

1 tsp white wine vinegar
1 small garlic clove, crushed
4 tbsp extra virgin olive oil
salt and pepper

method

1 Bring a large pan of water to a boil. Add the beans, bring back to a boil, then cook for 3 minutes, until just tender. Drain and tip into a serving dish or arrange on individual plates.

2 Whisk together the dressing ingredients and spoon over the beans while still warm.

3 Scatter over the diced tomato, basil, and Parmesan shavings. Serve immediately, at room temperature, in a warmed bowl.

bean sprout salad

ingredients

SERVES 4

4 cups bean sprouts

1 small cucumber

1 green bell pepper, seeded
      and cut into matchsticks

1 carrot, cut into matchsticks

2 tomatoes, finely chopped

1 celery stalk, cut into
      matchsticks

fresh chives, to garnish

dressing

1 garlic clove, crushed

dash of chili sauce

2 tbsp light soy sauce

1 tsp wine vinegar

2 tsp sesame oil

method

1 Blanch the bean sprouts in boiling water for 1 minute. Drain well, rinse under cold water, then drain again.

2 Cut the cucumber in half lengthwise. Scoop out the seeds with a teaspoon and discard. Cut the flesh into matchsticks with a sharp knife and mix with the bean sprouts, green bell pepper, carrot, tomatoes, and celery in a large bowl.

3 To make the dressing, mix together the crushed garlic, chilli sauce, soy sauce, wine vinegar, and sesame oil in a small bowl. Pour the dressing over the vegetables, tossing well to thoroughly coat the salad.

4 Spoon the salad onto 4 individual serving plates. Garnish with fresh chives and serve immediately.

indonesian warm salad

ingredients

SERVES 4

8 outer leaves of romaine
    lettuce or similar dark,
    crisp lettuce leaves
$3^1/_2$ oz/100 g green beans,
    lightly cooked
$3^1/_2$ oz/100 g baby carrots,
    lightly cooked
9 oz/250 g new potatoes,
    cooked until just tender
1 tbsp peanut oil
generous $3/_4$ cup fresh bean
    sprouts
$3^1/_4$-inch/8-cm piece
    cucumber, seeded and
    cut into $1^1/_2$-inch/4-cm
    matchsticks
4 hard-cooked eggs
1 small mild onion, sliced into
    rings

dressing

4 tbsp canned coconut milk
3 tbsp smooth peanut butter
juice of $1/_2$ lime
2 tsp light soy sauce
dash of Tabasco sauce or any
    chili sauce

method

1 Roughly tear the lettuce leaves, if large, and arrange on 4 individual serving plates or 1 large serving platter. Halve the beans and cut the carrots, as necessary, into matchsticks. Arrange these with the potatoes (cut into chunks if large) on the plates or platter.

2 Heat the oil in a nonstick skillet or wok over high heat, then add the bean sprouts and stir-fry for 2 minutes, or until lightly cooked or still crisp. Remove with a slotted spoon and sprinkle over the cooked vegetables with the cucumber. Peel and quarter the eggs, then arrange on top of the salad.

3 Add the onion rings to the oil remaining in the skillet or wok and stir-fry over high heat for 5 minutes, or until golden and crisp.

4 To make the dressing, combine the ingredients in a small bowl and pour over the salad. Top with the onion rings and serve immediately.

cauliflower, broccoli & cashew salad

ingredients

SERVES 4

2 tbsp peanut oil or
vegetable oil

2 red onions, cut into wedges

1 small head cauliflower,
cut into florets

1 small head broccoli,
cut into florets

2 tbsp prepared yellow curry
paste or red curry paste

1³/₄ cups canned coconut
milk

1 tsp Thai fish sauce

1 tsp jaggery

1 tsp salt

¹/₂ cup unsalted cashew nuts

handful of fresh cilantro,
chopped, plus extra
sprigs, torn, to garnish

method

1 Heat the oil in a preheated wok. Add the onions and stir-fry over medium–high heat for 3–4 minutes, or until starting to brown. Add the cauliflower and broccoli and stir-fry for 1–2 minutes. Stir in the curry paste and stir-fry for 30 seconds, then add the coconut milk, fish sauce, jaggery, and salt. Bring gently to a boil, stirring occasionally, then reduce the heat and simmer gently for 3–4 minutes, or until the vegetables are almost tender.

2 Meanwhile, heat a separate dry skillet until hot. Add the nuts and cook, shaking the skillet frequently, for 2–3 minutes, or until lightly browned. Add to the stir-fry with the cilantro and stir well, then serve immediately, garnished with torn sprigs of cilantro.

lentil & goat cheese salad

ingredients

SERVES 4

2 tbsp Puy lentils

1 bay leaf

2 scallions, finely chopped

scant $1/4$ cup diced red bell
   pepper

1 tbsp chopped fresh parsley

$3^1/2$ oz/100 g cherry
   tomatoes, halved

$1/3$ cup arugula

1 oz/25 g goat cheese, sliced
   or crumbled

dressing

1 tsp olive oil

1 tsp balsamic vinegar

$1/2$ tsp honey

1 garlic clove, crushed or
   finely chopped

method

1 Rinse the lentils and put in a medium-size pan. Add the bay leaf and cover with plenty of cold water. Bring to a boil, then reduce the heat and simmer for 20–30 minutes, or until the lentils are tender.

2 Drain the lentils and transfer to a bowl. Add the scallions, bell pepper, parsley, and cherry tomatoes. Mix well.

3 To make the dressing, whisk together the oil, vinegar, honey, and garlic and stir into the lentils. Serve on a bed of arugula, sprinkled with the goat cheese.

fruity cottage cheese salad

ingredients

SERVES 4

$^1/_3$ cup cottage cheese

1 tsp chopped fresh parsley

1 tbsp snipped fresh chives

1 tsp chopped fresh chervil or basil

2 assorted colored bell peppers, seeded and peeled

1 small melon, such as ogen (about 10$^1/_2$ oz/300 g after peeling and seeding)

6 oz/175 g assorted salad greens

2 oz/55 g seedless grapes

1 red onion, thinly sliced

dressing

3 tbsp freshly squeezed lime juice

1 small fresh red chile, seeded and finely chopped

1 tsp honey

1 tbsp soy sauce

method

1 Place the cottage cheese in a bowl and stir in the chopped herbs. Cover lightly and set aside.

2 Cut the peeled bell peppers into thin strips and set aside. Cut the melon in half, discard the seeds, and cut into small wedges. Remove and discard the rind, or run a sharp knife between the skin and flesh to loosen, then cut the flesh horizontally across. Push the flesh in alternate directions but so that it still sits on the skin. Set aside.

3 Arrange the salad greens on a large serving platter with the melon wedges.

4 Spoon the herb-flavored cottage cheese on the platter and arrange the reserved bell peppers, grapes, and red onion slices around the cheese.

5 To make the dressing, mix the lime juice, chile, honey, and soy sauce together in a small bowl or pitcher, then drizzle over the salad and serve as 4 portions.

warm asian-style salad

ingredients

SERVES 4

4 oz/115 g broccoli florets

4 oz/115 g baby carrots,
  scraped and cut in half
  lengthwise

5 oz/140 g bok choy

2 sprays sunflower oil

1 red onion, sliced

1–2 fresh Thai chiles, seeded
  and sliced

1-inch/2.5-cm piece fresh
  ginger, peeled and grated

2 whole star anise

1 red bell pepper, seeded and
  cut into strips

1 orange bell pepper, seeded
  and cut into strips

4 oz/115 g baby zucchini,
  trimmed and sliced
  diagonally

4 oz/115 g baby corn, sliced
  in half lengthwise

2 tbsp orange juice

1 tbsp soy sauce

1 tbsp cashew nuts

method

1 Cut the broccoli into tiny florets, then bring a small pan of water to a boil and add the halved carrots. Cook for 3 minutes, then add the broccoli and cook for an additional 2 minutes. Drain and plunge into cold water, then drain again and set aside.

2 Arrange 1 oz/25 g of the bok choy on a large serving platter. Shred the remainder and set aside.

3 Heat a wok and when hot, add the oil and heat for 30 seconds. Add the sliced onion, chiles, ginger, and star anise and stir-fry for 1 minute. Add the bell pepper strips, zucchini, and baby corn and stir-fry for an additional 2 minutes.

4 Pour in the orange juice and soy sauce and continue to stir-fry for 1 minute before adding the reserved shredded bok choy. Stir-fry for 2 minutes, or until the vegetables are tender but still firm to the bite. Arrange the warm salad on the bok choy-lined serving platter, scatter the cashew nuts over the top, and serve as 4 portions.

moroccan tomato & red pepper salad

ingredients

SERVES 4

3 red bell peppers

4 ripe tomatoes

1/2 bunch of fresh cilantro, chopped

2 garlic cloves, finely chopped

salt and pepper

method

1 Preheat the broiler. Place the bell peppers on a baking sheet and cook under the broiler, turning occasionally, for 15 minutes. Add the tomatoes and broil, turning occasionally, for an additional 5 to 10 minutes, or until all the skins are charred and blistered. Remove from the heat and let cool.

2 Peel and seed the bell peppers and tomatoes and slice the flesh thinly. Place in a bowl, mix well, and season with salt and pepper. Sprinkle with the cilantro and garlic, cover with plastic wrap, and chill in the refrigerator for at least 1 hour. Just before serving, drain off any excess liquid.

wilted spinach, yogurt & walnut salad

ingredients

SERVES 2

1 lb/450 g fresh spinach
    leaves
1 onion, chopped
1 tbsp olive oil
1 cup plain yogurt
1 garlic clove, finely chopped
2 tbsp chopped toasted
    walnuts
2–3 tsp chopped fresh mint
salt and pepper
pita bread, to serve

method

1 Put the spinach and onion into a pan, cover, and cook gently for a few minutes, until the spinach has wilted.

2 Add the oil and cook for an additional 5 minutes. Season with salt and pepper to taste.

3 Combine the yogurt and garlic in a bowl.

4 Put the spinach and onion into a serving bowl and pour over the yogurt mixture. Scatter over the walnuts and chopped mint and serve with pita bread.

moroccan carrot & orange salad

ingredients

SERVES 4

1 lb/450 g carrots, peeled

2 large oranges, peeled and
   cut into segments (reserve
   any juice)

$1/3$ cup raisins

1 tsp ground cinnamon

2 tbsp toasted pine nuts

dressing

1 tbsp olive oil

2 tbsp lemon juice

pinch of granulated sugar

method

1 Grate the carrots into a large bowl.

2 To make the dressing, in a separate bowl, combine the oil, lemon juice, sugar, and any orange juice reserved from the preparing of the orange segments.

3 Toss the orange segments with the carrots and stir in the raisins and cinnamon.

4 Pour over the dressing and scatter over the pine nuts just before serving.

hot tomato & basil salad

ingredients

SERVES 6

$1^{1}/_{2}$ lb/700 g cherry tomatoes

1 garlic clove, crushed

2 tbsp capers, drained and
  rinsed

1 tsp granulated sugar

4 tbsp olive oil

2 tbsp torn fresh basil

fresh crusty bread, to serve

method

1 Preheat the oven to 400°F/200°C. Stir the tomatoes, garlic, capers, and sugar together in a bowl and tip into a roasting pan.

2 Pour over the oil and toss to coat.

3 Cook in the oven for 10 minutes, until the tomatoes are hot.

4 Remove from the oven and tip into a heatproof serving bowl. Scatter over the basil and serve immediately with fresh crusty bread.

sweet & sour cabbage salad

ingredients

SERVES 6

$1/2$ cup fish sauce

$1/2$ cup freshly squeezed lime
   juice

$1/2$ cup jaggery or granulated
   sugar

2 tbsp vegetable oil

3 red chiles, seeded and
   thinly sliced into circles

1 small green cabbage, finely
   shredded (6 cups prepared)

2 large carrots, cut into thin
   sticks

1 small red onion, finely
   sliced

12 large fresh basil leaves,
   freshly torn, or $1/2$ cup
   fresh cilantro leaves

method

1 Put the fish sauce, lime juice, and sugar in a
nonreactive bowl and whisk until the sugar is
completely dissolved. Add the oil, chiles,
cabbage, carrots, and onion. Toss well and let
stand for 30 minutes to 1 hour.

2 Drain and serve scattered with the basil.

green papaya salad

ingredients

SERVES 6

$^1/_2$ cup freshly squeezed lime
   juice

$^1/_3$ cup fish sauce

$^1/_3$ cup jaggery or granulated
   sugar

1 large green papaya, peeled,
   seeded, and cut into
   very fine matchsticks
   (4–6 cups prepared)

2 small carrots, peeled and
   cut into matchsticks

3 red chiles, seeded and
   thinly sliced into circles

$^1/_2$ cup dry-roasted, unsalted
   peanuts, chopped

$^1/_2$ cup fresh cilantro leaves,
   or 12 fresh basil leaves,
   freshly torn

method

1 Put the lime juice, fish sauce, and sugar in
a nonreactive bowl and whisk until the sugar
is completely dissolved. Add the papaya,
carrots, and chiles. Toss well and let stand
for 30 minutes.

2 Drain and serve scattered with the peanuts
and cilantro leaves.

tomato salad with fried feta

ingredients

SERVES 4

12 tomatoes, sliced

1 very small red onion, sliced
    very thinly

$1/2$ oz/15 g arugula leaves

20 Greek black olives

7 oz/200 g authentic Greek
    feta cheese

1 egg

3 tbsp all-purpose flour

2 tbsp olive oil

dressing

3 tbsp extra virgin olive oil

juice of $1/2$ lemon

2 tsp chopped fresh oregano

pinch of sugar

pepper

method

1 To make the dressing, whisk together the extra virgin olive oil, lemon juice, oregano, sugar, and pepper in a small bowl. Set aside.

2 Prepare the salad by arranging the tomatoes, onion, arugula, and olives on 4 individual plates.

3 Cut the feta cheese into cubes about 1-inch/ 2.5-cm square. Beat the egg in a dish and put the flour on a separate plate. Toss the cheese first in the egg, shake off the excess, and then toss in the flour.

4 Heat the olive oil in a large skillet, add the cheese, and fry over a medium heat, turning over the cubes of cheese until they are golden on all sides.

5 Scatter the fried feta over the salad. Whisk together the prepared dressing, spoon over the salad, and serve warm.

orange & olive salad

ingredients

SERVES 4

4 thick-skinned oranges

1 small red onion, sliced very
thinly

16 large black Greek olives,
pitted

2 tbsp extra virgin olive oil

1 tbsp lemon juice

pinch of sugar

lettuce leaves, to serve

chopped fresh herbs, such as
flat-leaved parsley, mint,
or dill, to garnish

salt and pepper

method

1 Using a sharp knife, remove the peel and pith from the oranges, then cut the flesh into 1/4-inch/5-mm thick slices, discarding the seeds and white membrane. Put the oranges and any juice, the onion slices, and the olives in a large bowl.

2 To make the dressing, whisk together the oil, lemon juice, sugar, and salt and pepper to taste and drizzle over the salad ingredients. Gently toss together, then chill in the refrigerator for 2–3 hours before serving in a shallow dish lined with lettuce leaves. Garnish with chopped fresh herbs.

charred bell pepper salad

ingredients

SERVES 4–6

2 green bell peppers
2 red bell peppers
2 yellow bell peppers
Greek olives, to garnish

dressing

$1/2$ tsp cumin seeds or 2 tbsp
      chopped fresh marjoram
5 tbsp extra virgin olive oil
2 tbsp lemon juice
2 garlic cloves, crushed
pinch of sugar
salt and pepper

method

1 Preheat the broiler. Broil the bell peppers, turning frequently, until the skins are charred all over. Put the bell peppers in a bowl, cover with a damp dish towel, and let stand until cold.

2 When the bell peppers are cold, hold them over a clean bowl to collect the juices and peel off the skin. Remove the stem, core, and seeds and cut the peppers into thin strips. Arrange the bell pepper strips on a flat serving plate.

3 If using cumin seeds, dry-toast them in a dry skillet until they turn brown and begin to pop. Shake the skillet continuously to prevent them from burning and do not allow them to smoke. Lightly crush the toasted seeds with a pestle and mortar.

4 To make the dressing, add the toasted cumin seeds, olive oil, lemon juice, garlic, sugar, and salt and pepper to taste, to the bell pepper juices and whisk together.

5 Pour the dressing over the bell peppers and chill in the refrigerator for 3–4 hours or overnight. Serve at room temperature, garnished with olives.

hot-&-sour vegetable salad

ingredients

SERVES 4

2 tbsp vegetable or peanut oil

1 tbsp chili oil

1 onion, sliced

1-inch piece ginger, grated

1 small head broccoli, cut
　　into florets

2 carrots, cut into short thin
　　sticks

1 red bell pepper, seeded and
　　cut into squares

1 yellow bell pepper, seeded
　　and cut into strips

2 oz/55 g of snow peas,
　　trimmed

2 oz/55 g baby corn, halved

dressing

2 tbsp vegetable or peanut oil

1 tsp chili oil

1 tbsp rice wine vinegar

juice of 1 lime

$1/2$ tsp fish sauce

method

1 Heat the oils in a wok or large skillet and sauté the onion and ginger for 1–2 minutes, until they start to soften. Add the vegetables and stir-fry for 2–3 minutes, until they have softened slightly. Remove from the heat and set aside.

2 Mix the dressing ingredients together. Transfer the vegetables to a serving plate and drizzle the dressing over. Serve warm immediately, or let the flavors develop and serve cold.

curried egg salad

ingredients

SERVES 4

6 eggs

1 tbsp vegetable or peanut oil

1 onion, chopped

1 tbsp yellow curry paste

4 tbsp plain yogurt

$1/2$ tsp salt

handful of fresh cilantro,
    chopped finely

bunch of watercress or
    arugula

2 zucchini, cut into short,
    matchsticks

dressing

1 fresh green chile, seeded
    and chopped finely

1 tsp fish sauce

1 tsp rice wine vinegar

3 tbsp vegetable or peanut oil

method

1 Put the eggs in a pan, cover with cold water, and bring to a boil. Let simmer for 10 minutes, then drain and rinse in cold water. Shell and halve.

2 Meanwhile, heat the oil in a medium skillet and sauté the onion gently until softened but not browned. Remove from the heat and stir in the curry paste. Let cool slightly before stirring in the yogurt, salt, and half the cilantro. Set aside.

3 Arrange the watercress and zucchini on a platter. To make the dressing, mix together the green chile, fish sauce, vinegar, and oil and pour over the salad leaves.

4 Arrange the egg halves on top of the dressed salad leaves and spoon the yogurt mixture on top. Garnish with the remaining cilantro and serve.

julienne vegetable salad

ingredients

SERVES 4

4 tbsp vegetable or peanut oil

8 oz tofu with herbs, cubed

1 red onion, sliced

4 scallions, cut into
    2-inch/5-cm lengths

1 garlic clove, chopped

2 carrots, cut into short,
    matchsticks

4 oz/115 g fine green beans,
    trimmed

1 yellow bell pepper, seeded
    and cut into strips

4 oz/115 g broccoli, cut into
    florets

1 large zucchini, cut into
    short, matchsticks

1/2 cup bean sprouts

2 tbsp red curry paste

4 tbsp Thai soy sauce

1 tbsp rice wine vinegar

1 tsp jaggery or light brown
    sugar

few basil leaves, plus extra to
    garnish (optional)

12 oz/350 g rice vermicelli
    noodles

method

1 Heat the oil in a wok or large skillet and cook the tofu cubes for 3–4 minutes, until browned on all sides. Lift out of the oil and drain on paper towels.

2 Add the onions, garlic, and carrots to the hot oil and cook for 1–2 minutes before adding the rest of the vegetables, except for the bean sprouts. Stir-fry for 2–3 minutes. Add the bean sprouts, then stir in the curry paste, soy sauce, vinegar, sugar, and basil leaves. Cook for 30 seconds.

3 Soak the noodles in boiling water or stock for 2–3 minutes (check the package instructions) or until tender, and drain well.

4 Pile the vegetables onto the noodles, and serve topped with the tofu cubes. Garnish with extra basil if desired.

eggplant & onion salad

ingredients

SERVES 4

4 tbsp vegetable or peanut oil

1 onion, sliced

4 shallots, chopped finely

4 scallions, sliced

12 oz/350 g eggplants, cubed

2 tbsp green curry paste

2 tbsp soy sauce

1 tsp jaggery or light brown
  sugar

4 oz/115 g block creamed
  coconut, chopped

3 tbsp water

small handful of fresh
  cilantro, chopped

few basil leaves, chopped

small handful of fresh parsley,
  chopped

2$\frac{1}{2}$ cups arugula leaves

2 tbsp sweet chili sauce

method

1 Heat half the oil in a wok or large skillet and cook all the onions together for 1–2 minutes, until just softened but not browned. Lift out and set aside.

2 Cook the eggplant cubes, in batches if necessary, adding more oil as needed, until they are crisp and golden brown.

3 Return the onions to the wok and add the curry paste, soy sauce, and sugar. Add the creamed coconut and water and cook until dissolved. Stir in most of the cilantro, the basil, and the parsley.

4 Toss the arugula in the chili sauce and serve with the eggplant and onion salad. Garnish with the remaining herbs.

chinese tomato salad

ingredients

SERVES 4–6

2 large tomatoes

dressing

1 tbsp finely chopped scallion

1 tsp finely chopped garlic

$1/2$ tsp sesame oil

1 tbsp white rice vinegar

$1/2$ tsp salt

pinch of white pepper

pinch of sugar

method

1 Mix together all the ingredients for the dressing and set aside.

2 Thinly slice the tomatoes. Arrange on a plate and pour the dressing over the top.

beet salad

ingredients

SERVES 4–6

2 lb/900 g raw beets

dressing

4 tbsp extra virgin olive oil

1$\frac{1}{2}$ tbsp red wine vinegar

2 garlic cloves, finely chopped

2 scallions, chopped

coarse sea salt

method

1 Carefully remove the roots from the beets without cutting into the skin, then cut off all but 1 inch/2.5 cm of the stalks. Gently rub the beets under cold running water, without splitting the skins, to remove any dirt. Put the beets in a saucepan with enough water to cover and bring to a boil. Cover, reduce the heat slightly, and cook for 25–40 minutes, depending on the size, until the largest beet is tender when you pierce it with a long metal skewer or knife.

2 To make the dressing, put the oil, vinegar, garlic, scallions, and salt to taste in a jar with a screw-top lid and shake until emulsified. Set aside.

3 Drain the beets and rinse under cold running water until cool enough to handle, then peel away the skins. Thickly chop or slice the beets, then put in a bowl and pour over the dressing. Cover and chill in the refrigerator for at least 1 hour.

4 To serve, gently toss the salad and transfer to a serving platter.

watercress, zucchini & mint salad

ingredients

SERVES 4

2 zucchini, cut into
matchsticks

3^{1}/$_{2}$ oz/100 g green beans,
cut into thirds

1 green bell pepper, seeded
and cut into strips

2 celery stalks, sliced

1 bunch of watercress

salt

dressing

scant 1 cup plain yogurt

1 garlic clove, crushed

2 tbsp chopped fresh mint

pepper

method

1 Bring a saucepan of lightly salted water to a boil, add the zucchini matchsticks and beans, and cook for 7–8 minutes. Drain, rinse under cold running water, and drain again. Set aside to cool completely.

2 Mix the zucchini and beans with the bell pepper strips, celery, and watercress in a large serving bowl.

3 To make the dressing, combine the yogurt, garlic, and mint in a small bowl. Season with pepper to taste.

4 Spoon the dressing onto the salad and serve immediately.

poultry & meat salads

There is a world of difference between serving, say, chicken with salad and creating a genuine chicken salad. For a truly delicious, attractive, and appetizing dish, the meat or poultry needs to be an integral part of the salad and combine perfectly with the other ingredients, whether vegetables, nuts, herbs, fruit, pasta, or rice.

Virtually all kinds of poultry and meat make terrific salads. Chicken and turkey go especially well with creamy mixtures, duck is delicious with piquant flavors, bacon and pancetta have a natural affinity with peppery greens and the earthy taste of mushrooms, while beef works equally well with both western and eastern culinary traditions. Duck, bacon, and beef, in particular, are superb in warm salads.

Serving a main-course salad made with meat or poultry is not only a good way to add variety to the family menu in the winter as well as the summer, but an easy route to a healthy diet. You are more or less guaranteed a balanced and nutritious meal with protein, vitamins, minerals, fiber, and, if the salad includes potatoes, noodles, pasta, or rice, carbohydrates too. If not, serve it with crusty rolls or fresh bread—delicious.

chicken avocado salad

ingredients

SERVES 4

4 large handfuls mixed salad
  greens, such as beet
  greens, escarole, endive,
  and radicchio
14 oz/400 g boneless,
  skinless cooked chicken,
  cut into bite-size pieces
2 satsumas, separated into
  segments
2 celery stalks, thinly sliced
$^1/_2$ red onion, halved and
  thinly sliced
2 tbsp snipped fresh chives
2 avocados
2 tbsp toasted sunflower
  seeds, to garnish
pita bread, to serve

dressing

$^1/_2$ cup extra virgin olive oil
3 tbsp Chinese rice wine
  vinegar
$^1/_2$ tsp Dijon mustard
pinch of superfine sugar
salt and pepper

method

1 To make the dressing, put the oil, vinegar, mustard, sugar, and salt and pepper to taste into a small screw-top jar and shake until blended and emulsified.

2 Put the salad greens into a bowl, add about one third of the dressing, and lightly toss. Add the chicken, satsumas, celery, onion, chives, and the remaining dressing and toss again.

3 Cut the avocados in half and remove the pit, then peel away the skin. Cut the flesh into thin slices, add to the other ingredients, and gently toss together, making sure the avocado slices are completely coated with dressing so they don't discolor.

4 Arrange on individual plates, sprinkle with sunflower seeds, and serve with pita bread on the side.

cajun chicken salad

ingredients

SERVES 4

4 skinless, boneless chicken
    breasts, about 5 oz/140 g
    each
4 tsp Cajun seasoning
2 tsp corn oil (optional)
1 ripe mango, peeled,
    seeded, and cut into thick
    slices
7 oz/200 g mixed salad
    greens
1 red onion, thinly sliced and
    cut in half
6 oz/175 g cooked beet,
    diced
3 oz/85 g radishes, sliced
generous 3/8 cup walnut halves
2 tbsp sesame seeds,
    to garnish

dressing
4 tbsp walnut oil
1–2 tsp Dijon mustard
1 tbsp lemon juice
salt and pepper

method

1 Make 3 diagonal slashes across each chicken breast. Put the chicken into a shallow dish and sprinkle all over with the Cajun seasoning. Cover and let chill for at least 30 minutes.

2 When ready to cook, brush a stove-top grill pan with the corn oil, if using. Heat over high heat until very hot and a few drops of water sprinkled into the pan sizzle immediately. Add the chicken and cook for 7–8 minutes on each side, or until thoroughly cooked. If still slightly pink in the center, cook a little longer. Remove the chicken and set aside.

3 Add the mango slices to the pan and cook for 2 minutes on each side. Remove and set aside.

4 Meanwhile, arrange the salad greens in a salad bowl and sprinkle over the onion, beet, radishes, and walnut halves.

5 Put the walnut oil, mustard, lemon juice, and salt and pepper to taste in a screw-top jar and shake until well blended. Pour over the salad.

6 Arrange the mango and the salad on the serving plate, top with the chicken breast, and sprinkle with sesame seeds.

roast chicken with pesto cream salad

ingredients

SERVES 4–6

1 lb 5 oz/600 g cooked
   boneless chicken, any
   skin removed and cut into
   bite-size chunks
3 celery stalks, chopped
2 large, skinned red bell
   peppers from a jar, well
   drained and sliced
salt and pepper
iceberg lettuce leaves,
   to serve

pesto cream

2/3 cup sour cream
about 4 tbsp bottled pesto
   sauce

method

1 To make the pesto cream, put the sour cream into a large bowl, then beat in 4 tablespoons pesto sauce. Taste and add more pesto if you want a stronger flavor.

2 Add the chicken, celery, and bell peppers to the bowl and gently toss together. Add salt and pepper to taste and toss again. Cover and chill until required.

3 Remove the salad from the refrigerator 10 minutes before serving to return to room temperature. Give the salad ingredients a good stir, then divide among individual plates lined with lettuce leaves.

braised chicken salad

ingredients

SERVES 4

3 tbsp olive oil

1 chicken, weighing about
   3 lb/1.3 kg

scant 1 cup dry white wine

1 onion, chopped

1 carrot, chopped

1 celery stalk, chopped

1 fresh bay leaf

salt and pepper

marinade

1 tsp black peppercorns

4 fresh bay leaves

$1/2$ cup olive oil

salt

salad

$5^1/2$ oz/150 g baby spinach
   leaves

5 tender celery stalks

1 head chicory

1 tsp wine vinegar

1 tsp balsamic vinegar

salt

method

1 Preheat the oven to 350°F/180°C. Heat the olive oil in an ovenproof casserole over medium–high heat. Add the chicken and fry for 15 minutes, turning, until golden all over. Pour in the wine and simmer for 2 minutes, then add the onion, carrot, celery, and bay leaf. Season with salt and pepper. Cover tightly and transfer to the oven. Bake for 45–50 minutes, turning every 20 minutes, until the juices from the thickest part of the thigh run clear when pierced with a skewer. Discard the liquid and solids. When cool enough to handle, remove and discard the skin. Strip the meat from the bone, slicing any large chunks into bite-size pieces.

2 To marinate the chicken, arrange it in a dish. Sprinkle with a little salt, a few peppercorns, and the bay leaves. Pour in enough oil to generously coat. Cover tightly with plastic wrap and let stand in the refrigerator for 1–2 days. Remove the chicken from the refrigerator 2 hours before serving. Place in a colander set over a bowl to drain, and let stand until the oil has liquefied.

3 To make the salad, chop the leaves as desired. Combine the spinach, celery, and chicory in a large serving dish. Toss with salt, enough oil from the chicken to just coat the leaves, and the wine vinegar. Arrange the chicken on top, discarding the peppercorns and bay leaves. Sprinkle with the balsamic vinegar before serving.

thai chicken salad

ingredients

SERVES 6

1 tbsp vegetable oil

4 oz/115 g skinless chicken
   breast portion, cut
   lengthwise horizontally

1 oz/25 g rice vermicelli

spicy dressing of your choice

3 limes, halved

salad

$1/2$ cup seeded, mixed bell
   peppers, sliced into thin
   strips

$1/3$ cup thin carrot strips

$1/3$ cup thin zucchini strips

$1/3$ cup thin snow pea strips

scant $1/2$ cup baby corn cobs,
   sliced into thin strips

$1/2$ cup broccoli florets, cut
   into $1/4$-inch/5-mm pieces

$1/2$ cup shredded bok choy

4 tbsp coarsely chopped
   fresh cilantro leaves

method

1 Heat the oil in a stove-top grill pan over high heat. Add the chicken and cook for 2 minutes on each side, or until thoroughly cooked through. Remove the chicken from the pan and shred.

2 Cook the vermicelli according to the package instructions.

3 To make the salad, put all the salad ingredients with the chicken into a large bowl. Drain the vermicelli and add to the bowl. Pour the dressing over the salad and toss together, making sure that all the ingredients are well coated. Cover and chill in the refrigerator for at least 2 hours before serving. Serve on large plates, squeezing the juice from half a lime over each serving.

layered chicken salad

ingredients

SERVES 4

1 lb 10 oz/750 g new
  potatoes, scrubbed
1 red bell pepper, halved and
  seeded
1 green bell pepper, halved
  and seeded
2 small zucchini, sliced
1 small onion, thinly sliced
3 tomatoes, sliced
12 oz/350 g cooked chicken,
  sliced
chopped fresh chives,
  to garnish

dressing

$^2/_3$ cup plain yogurt
3 tbsp mayonnaise
1 tbsp chopped fresh chives
salt and pepper

method

1 Put the potatoes into a large pan, add just enough cold water to cover, and bring to a boil. Lower the heat, cover, and simmer for 15–20 minutes, until tender. Meanwhile, place the bell pepper halves, skin side up, under a preheated hot broiler and broil until the skins blacken and begin to char.

2 Remove the bell peppers with tongs, place in a bowl, and cover with plastic wrap. Set aside until cool enough to handle, then peel off the skins and slice the flesh.

3 Bring a small pan of lightly salted water to a boil. Add the zucchini, bring back to a boil, and simmer for 3 minutes. Drain, rinse under cold running water to prevent any additional cooking, and drain again. Set aside.

4 To make the dressing, whisk the yogurt, mayonnaise, and chopped chives together in a small bowl until well blended. Season to taste with salt and pepper.

5 When the potatoes are tender, drain, cool, and slice them. Add them to the dressing and mix gently to coat evenly. Spoon the potatoes onto 4 serving plates, dividing them equally.

6 Top each plate with one quarter of the bell pepper slices and zucchini. Layer one-quarter of the onion and tomato slices, then the sliced chicken, on top of each serving. Garnish with chopped chives and serve immediately.

turkey salad pita

ingredients

MAKES 1

small handful baby leaf
    spinach, rinsed, patted
    dry, and shredded
$1/2$ red bell pepper, seeded
    and thinly sliced
$1/2$ carrot, peeled and coarsely
    grated
4 tbsp hummus
3 oz/85 g boneless, skinless
    cooked turkey meat, thinly
    sliced
$1/2$ tbsp toasted sunflower
    seeds
1 whole-wheat pita
salt and pepper

method

1 Preheat the broiler to high.

2 Put the spinach leaves, bell pepper, carrot, and hummus into a large bowl and stir together, so all the salad ingredients are coated with the hummus. Stir in the turkey and sunflower seeds and season to taste with salt and pepper.

3 Put the pita under the broiler for about 1 minute on each side to warm through, but do not brown. Cut it in half to make 2 "pockets" of bread.

4 Divide the salad among the pita pockets and serve.

turkey & rice salad

ingredients

SERVES 4

4 cups chicken stock

scant 1 cup mixed long-grain
   and wild rice

2 tbsp corn oil

8 oz/225 g skinless, boneless
   turkey breast, trimmed of
   all visible fat and cut into
   thin strips

2 cups snow peas

4 oz/115 g oyster mushrooms,
   torn into pieces

1/4 cup shelled pistachio nuts,
   finely chopped

2 tbsp chopped fresh cilantro

1 tbsp snipped fresh garlic
   chives

1 tbsp balsamic vinegar

salt and pepper

fresh garlic chives, to garnish

method

1 Set aside 3 tablespoons of the chicken stock and bring the remainder to a boil in a large pan. Add the rice and cook for 30 minutes, or until tender. Drain and let cool slightly.

2 Meanwhile, heat 1 tablespoon of the oil in a preheated wok or skillet. Stir-fry the turkey over medium heat for 3–4 minutes, or until cooked through. Using a slotted spoon, transfer the turkey to a dish. Add the snow peas and mushrooms to the wok and stir-fry for 1 minute. Add the reserved stock, bring to a boil, then reduce the heat, cover, and let simmer for 3–4 minutes. Transfer the vegetables to the dish and let cool slightly.

3 Thoroughly mix the rice, turkey, snow peas, mushrooms, nuts, cilantro, and garlic chives together, then season to taste with salt and pepper. Drizzle with the remaining corn oil and the vinegar and garnish with fresh garlic chives. Serve warm.

warm duck salad

ingredients

SERVES 4

6 oz/175 g duck breast,
   all fat removed

1 tbsp sunflower oil

1-inch/2.5-cm piece fresh
   ginger, peeled and grated

1 fresh serrano chile, seeded
   and sliced

1 red onion, cut into thin
   wedges

2 celery stalks, trimmed and
   finely sliced

1 small red bell pepper,
   seeded and finely sliced

1 tbsp soy sauce

4 oz/115 g zucchini, trimmed
   and sliced

2 ripe but still firm plums,
   pitted and sliced

3 oz/85 g bok choy, shredded

1 tbsp chopped fresh cilantro

method

1 Cut the duck breast into thin strips and set aside. Heat a wok until very hot, then add the oil, and heat for 30 seconds. Add the ginger, chile, and duck strips and stir-fry for 1–2 minutes, or until the duck strips are browned.

2 Add the onion wedges, celery, and pepper slices and continue to stir-fry for 3 minutes.

3 Add the soy sauce, zucchini, and plums to the wok and stir-fry for 2 minutes before stirring in the shredded bok choy and the chopped cilantro. Stir-fry for an additional minute, then serve, divided equally among 4 bowls.

asian duck & noodle salad with peanut sauce

ingredients

SERVES 3

2 carrots, peeled

2 celery stalks

1 cucumber

three 5 oz/140 g duck breasts

12 oz/350 g rice noodles,
     cooked according to
     directions on package,
     rinsed, and drained

peanut sauce

2 garlic cloves, crushed

2 tbsp dark brown sugar

2 tbsp peanut butter

2 tbsp coconut cream

2 tbsp soy sauce

2 tbsp rice vinegar

2 tbsp sesame oil

$1/2$ tsp freshly ground black
     pepper

$1/2$ tsp Chinese five-spice
     powder

$1/2$ tsp ground ginger

method

1 Preheat the broiler. Cut the carrots, celery, and cucumber into thin strips and set aside.

2 Broil the duck breasts for about 5 minutes on each side until cooked through. Let cool.

3 Meanwhile, heat all the ingredients for the sauce in a small pan until combined and the sugar has dissolved completely. Stir until smooth.

4 Slice the duck breasts. Divide the noodles among 3 serving bowls. Place the reserved carrots, celery, and cucumber on top of the noodles, arrange the duck slices on top, and drizzle with the sauce. Serve immediately.

duck & radish salad

ingredients

SERVES 4

12 oz boneless duck breasts

2 tbsp all-purpose flour

1 egg

2 tbsp water

2 tbsp sesame seeds

3 tbsp sesame oil

1/2 head Chinese cabbage, shredded

3 celery stalks, sliced finely

8 radishes, trimmed and halved

salt and pepper

fresh basil leaves, to garnish

dressing

finely grated peel of 1 lime

2 tbsp lime juice

2 tbsp olive oil

1 tbsp light soy sauce

1 tbsp chopped fresh basil

salt and pepper

method

1 Put each duck breast between sheets of parchment paper or plastic wrap. Use a meat mallet or rolling pin to beat them out and flatten them slightly.

2 Sprinkle the flour onto a large plate and season with salt and pepper. Beat the egg and water together in a shallow bowl, then sprinkle the sesame seeds onto a separate plate.

3 Dip the duck breasts first into the seasoned flour, then into the egg mixture, and finally into the sesame seeds to coat the duck evenly.

4 Heat the sesame oil in a preheated wok or large skillet. Fry the duck breasts over a medium heat for about 8 minutes, turning once. To test whether they are cooked, insert a sharp knife into the thickest part—the juices should run clear. Lift them out and drain on paper towels.

5 To make the dressing for the salad, whisk together the lime peel and juice, olive oil, soy sauce, and chopped basil. Season with a little salt and pepper.

8 Arrange the Chinese cabbage, celery, and radishes on a serving plate. Slice the duck breasts thinly and place on top of the salad.

7 Drizzle with the dressing and garnish with fresh basil leaves. Serve at once.

melon, chorizo & artichoke salad

ingredients

SERVES 8

12 small globe artichokes

juice of $1/2$ lemon

2 tbsp olive oil

1 small orange-fleshed
   melon, such as
   cantaloupe

7 oz/200 g chorizo sausage,
   outer casing removed

fresh tarragon or flat-leaf
   parsley sprigs, to garnish

dressing

3 tbsp extra virgin olive oil

1 tbsp red wine vinegar

1 tsp prepared mustard

1 tbsp chopped fresh
   tarragon

salt and pepper

method

1 Prepare the artichokes by using kitchen scissors to cut off the outside layer of leaves and snip off the tough tips, then brush the cut surfaces of the artichokes with lemon juice to prevent discoloration. Carefully remove the choke (the mass of silky hairs) by pulling it out with your fingers or by scooping it out with a spoon. It is very important to remove all the choke on older artichokes, because the little barbs, if eaten, can irritate the throat. Cut the artichokes into fourths and brush them again with lemon juice.

2 Heat the olive oil in a large, heavy-bottom skillet. Add the prepared artichokes and cook, stirring frequently, for 5 minutes, or until the artichoke leaves are golden brown. Remove from the skillet, then transfer to a large serving bowl and let cool.

3 To prepare the melon, cut in half and scoop out the seeds with a spoon. Cut the flesh into bite-size cubes. Add to the cooled artichokes. Cut the chorizo into bite-size chunks and add to the melon and artichokes

4 To make the dressing, place all the ingredients in a small bowl and whisk together. Just before serving, pour the dressing over the prepared salad ingredients and toss together. Serve the salad garnished with tarragon or parsley sprigs.

lima bean, onion & herb salad with spicy sausage

ingredients

SERVES 2

1 tbsp corn oil

1 small onion, finely sliced

9 oz/250 g canned lima beans, drained and rinsed

1 tsp balsamic vinegar

2 chorizo sausages, sliced diagonally

1 small tomato, diced

2 tbsp harissa paste

3 oz/85 g mixed herb leaves

method

1 Heat the oil in a nonstick skillet over medium heat, add the onion, and cook, stirring frequently, until softened but not browned. Add the beans and cook for 1 minute, then add the vinegar, stirring well. Keep warm.

2 Meanwhile, heat a separate dry skillet over medium heat, add the chorizo slices, and cook, turning occasionally, until lightly browned. Remove with a slotted spoon and drain on paper towels.

3 Mix the tomato and harissa paste together in a small bowl. Divide the herb leaves between 2 plates, spoon over the bean mixture, and sprinkle over the warm chorizo slices. Top with a spoonful of the tomato and harissa mixture and serve at once.

crispy spinach & bacon

ingredients

SERVES 4

4 tbsp olive oil

4 strips of lean bacon, diced

1 thick slice of white bread,
    crusts removed, cut into
    cubes

1 lb/450 g fresh spinach,
    torn or shredded

method

1 Heat 2 tablespoons of the olive oil over high heat in a large skillet. Add the diced bacon to the skillet and cook for 3–4 minutes, or until crisp. Remove with a slotted spoon, draining carefully, and set aside.

2 Toss the cubes of bread in the fat remaining in the skillet over high heat for about 4 minutes, or until crisp and golden. Remove the croutons with a slotted spoon, draining carefully, and set them aside.

3 Add the remaining oil to the skillet and heat. Toss the spinach in the oil over high heat for about 3 minutes, or until it has just wilted. Turn into a serving bowl and sprinkle with the bacon and croutons. Serve immediately.

egg & bacon salad

ingredients

SERVES 4

1 tbsp sunflower oil
6–8 slices bacon, diced
1 cup fresh breadcrumbs
selection of salad greens, torn
6–8 hard-cooked eggs,
     quartered
12 black olives

dressing

2 tbsp white wine vinegar
5 tbsp extra virgin olive oil
1 tbsp whole-grain mustard
salt and pepper

method

1 Heat the sunflower oil in a skillet, add the bacon, and cook for about 5 minutes until crisp. Remove from the skillet.

2 Add the breadcrumbs to the skillet and cook over high heat until crisp and golden. Set aside.

3 Put the salad greens into a bowl with the eggs and olives and tip in the bacon.

4 For the dressing, whisk the vinegar, extra virgin olive oil, mustard, and salt and pepper to taste together in a bowl and pour over the salad.

5 Toss to mix, sprinkle with the crisp breadcrumbs, and serve immediately.

warm mushroom, spinach & pancetta salad

ingredients

SERVES 4

generous 6 cups fresh baby
   spinach leaves
2 tbsp olive oil
5¹/₂ oz/150 g pancetta
10 oz/280 g mixed wild
   mushrooms, sliced

dressing

5 tbsp olive oil
1 tbsp balsamic vinegar
1 tsp Dijon mustard
pinch of sugar
salt and pepper

method

1 To make the dressing, place the olive oil, vinegar, mustard, sugar, salt, and pepper in a small bowl and whisk together. Rinse the baby spinach under cold running water, then drain and place in a large salad bowl.

2 Heat the oil in a large skillet. Add the pancetta and cook for 3 minutes. Add the mushrooms and cook for 3–4 minutes, or until tender.

3 Pour the dressing into the skillet and immediately turn the cooked mixture and dressing into the bowl with the spinach. Toss until coated with the dressing and serve at once.

roast pork & pumpkin salad

ingredients

SERVES 4–6

1 small pumpkin, about
   3^1/$_2$ lb/1.6 kg
2 red onions, cut into wedges
olive oil
3^1/$_2$ oz/100 g green beans,
   trimmed and cut in half
1^1/$_4$ lb/600 g roast pork, any
   skin or rind removed and
   cut into bite-size chunks
large handful fresh arugula
   leaves
3^1/$_2$ oz/100 g feta cheese,
   drained and crumbled
2 tbsp toasted pine nuts
2 tbsp chopped fresh parsley
salt and pepper

vinaigrette

6 tbsp extra virgin olive oil
3 tbsp balsamic vinegar
^{1}/$_2$ tsp sugar
^{1}/$_2$ tsp Dijon, prepared English
   or whole-grain mustard
salt and pepper

method

1 Preheat the oven to 400°F/200°C. Cut the pumpkin in half, scoop out the seeds and fibers, and cut the flesh into wedges about 1^1/$_2$ inches/4 cm wide. Very lightly rub the pumpkin and onion wedges with the olive oil, place in a roasting pan, and roast for 25–30 minutes, until the pumpkin and onions are tender but holding their shape.

2 Meanwhile, bring a small pan of salted water to a boil. Add the green beans and blanch for 5 minutes, or until tender. Drain well and cool under cold running water to stop them cooking. Drain well and pat dry.

3 Remove the pumpkin and onion wedges from the oven as soon as they are tender-crisp and let cool completely. When the pumpkin is cool, peel and cut into bite-size pieces.

4 To make the vinaigrette, put the oil, vinegar, sugar, mustard, and salt and pepper to taste into a screw-top jar and shake until blended.

5 To assemble the salad, put the pumpkin, onions, beans, pork, arugula, feta, pine nuts, and parsley in a large bowl and gently toss together—be careful not to break up the pumpkin. Shake the dressing again, pour over the salad, and gently toss. Divide among individual bowls and serve.

broiled lamb with yogurt & herb dressing

ingredients

SERVES 4

2 tbsp sunflower oil, plus
　　extra for broiling the lamb
1 tbsp tomato paste
1/2 tbsp ground cumin
1 tsp lemon juice
1 garlic clove, crushed
pinch of cayenne pepper
1 lb 2 oz/500 g lamb neck
　　fillets, trimmed with
　　excess fat removed
salt and pepper
toasted sesame seeds and
　　sprigs of fresh parsley,
　　to garnish

dressing

2 tbsp fresh lemon juice
1 tsp honey
generous 1/3 cup thick plain
　　yogurt
2 tbsp finely shredded fresh
　　mint
2 tbsp chopped fresh parsley
1 tbsp finely snipped fresh
　　chives
salt and pepper

method

1 Mix the oil, tomato paste, cumin, lemon juice, garlic, cayenne, and salt and pepper to taste together in a nonmetallic bowl. Add the lamb and rub all over with the marinade. Cover the bowl and marinate in the refrigerator for at least 2 hours, but ideally overnight.

2 Meanwhile, to make the dressing, whisk the lemon juice and honey together until the honey dissolves. Whisk in the yogurt until well blended. Stir in the herbs and add salt and pepper to taste. Cover and chill until required.

3 Remove the lamb from the refrigerator 15 minutes before you are ready to cook. Heat the broiler to its highest setting and lightly brush the broiler rack with oil. Broil the lamb, turning it once, for 10 minutes for medium and 12 minutes for well done. Let the lamb cool completely, then cover and chill until required.

4 Thinly slice the lamb, then divide among 4 plates. Adjust the seasoning in the dressing, if necessary, then spoon over the lamb slices. Sprinkle with toasted sesame seeds, garnish with the parsley, and serve.

roast beef salad

ingredients

SERVES 4

1 lb 10 oz/750 g beef
   tenderloin, trimmed of
   any visible fat
2 tsp Worcestershire sauce
3 tbsp olive oil
14 oz/400 g green beans
3$^{1}/_{2}$ oz/100 g small pasta,
   such as orecchiette
2 red onions, finely sliced
1 large head radicchio,
   chopped
generous $^{1}/_{4}$ cup green olives,
   pitted
scant $^{1}/_{3}$ cup shelled
   hazelnuts, whole
pepper

dressing

1 tsp Dijon mustard
2 tbsp white wine vinegar
5 tbsp olive oil

method

1 Preheat the oven to 425°F/220°C. Rub the beef with pepper to taste and Worcestershire sauce. Heat 2 tablespoons of the oil in a small roasting pan over high heat, add the beef, and sear on all sides. Transfer the dish to the preheated oven and roast for 30 minutes. Remove and let cool.

2 Bring a large pan of water to a boil, add the beans, and cook for 5 minutes, or until just tender. Remove with a slotted spoon and refresh the beans under cold running water. Drain and put into a large bowl.

3 Return the bean cooking water to a boil, add the pasta, and cook for 11 minutes, or until tender. Drain, return to the pan, and toss with the remaining oil.

4 Add the pasta to the beans with the onions, radicchio leaves, olives, and hazelnuts, mix gently, and transfer to a serving bowl or dish. Arrange some thinly sliced beef on top.

5 To make the dressing, whisk the ingredients together in a separate bowl, then pour over the salad and serve at once with extra sliced beef.

warm beef niçoise

ingredients

SERVES 4

4 beef tenderloin steaks,
about 4 oz/115 g each,
trimmed of any visible fat

2 tbsp red wine vinegar

2 tbsp orange juice

2 tsp prepared English
mustard

2 eggs

6 oz/175 g new potatoes

4 oz/115 g green beans,
trimmed

6 oz/175 g mixed salad
greens, such as baby
spinach, arugula, and
mizuna

1 yellow bell pepper, seeded,
peeled, and cut into strips

6 oz/175 g cherry tomatoes,
halved

black olives, pitted, to garnish
(optional)

2 tsp extra virgin olive oil

method

1 Place the steaks in a shallow dish. Blend the vinegar with 1 tablespoon of orange juice and 1 teaspoon of mustard. Pour over the steaks, cover, then let stand in the refrigerator for at least 30 minutes. Turn over halfway through the marinating time.

2 Place the eggs in a pan and cover with cold water. Bring to a boil, then reduce the heat to a simmer and cook for 10 minutes. Remove and plunge the eggs into cold water. Once cold, shell and set aside.

3 Meanwhile, place the potatoes in a pan and cover with cold water. Bring to a boil, then cover and let simmer for 15 minutes, or until tender when pierced with a fork. Drain and set aside.

4 Bring a saucepan of water to the boil, add the beans and cook for 5 minutes, or until just tender. Drain, plunge into cold water, and drain again. Arrange the potatoes and beans on top of the salad leaves together with the bell pepper, cherry tomatoes, and olives, if using. Blend the remaining orange juice and mustard with the olive oil and set aside.

5 Heat a stove-top grill pan until smoking. Drain the steaks and cook for 3–5 minutes on each side or according to personal preference. Slice the steaks and arrange on top of the salad, then pour over the dressing and serve.

chili beef stir-fry salad

ingredients

SERVES 4

1 lb/450 g lean sirloin or
    top round steak
2 cloves garlic, crushed
1 tsp chili powder
$^1/_2$ tsp salt
1 tsp ground coriander
1 ripe avocado
2 tbsp sunflower oil
15 oz/425 g canned red
    kidney beans, drained
6 oz/175 g cherry tomatoes,
    halved
1 large packet tortilla chips
head of iceberg lettuce,
    shredded
fresh cilantro, chopped,
    to serve

method

1 Using a sharp knife, slice the beef into thin strips.

2 Place the garlic, chili powder, salt, and ground coriander in a large bowl and mix until well combined. Add the strips of beef to the mixture and toss well to coat all over.

3 Using a sharp knife, peel the avocado and remove the pit. Slice the avocado lengthwise and then crosswise to form small dice.

4 Heat the oil in large preheated wok. Add the beef and cook for 5 minutes, tossing frequently. Add the kidney beans, tomatoes, and avocado, and heat through.

5 Spoon the beef mixture into bowls, garnish with the fresh cilantro and serve with bowls of tortilla chips and iceberg lettuce.

charbroiled beef salad

ingredients

SERVES 4

scant ²/₃ cup dried oyster
    mushrooms

1 lb 5 oz/600 g sirloin or top
    round steak

2 red bell pepper, seeded and
    sliced thinly

generous ¹/₄ cup roasted
    cashew nuts

red and green lettuce leaves,
    to serve

mint leaves, to garnish

dressing

2 tbsp sesame oil

2 tbsp fish sauce

2 tbsp sweet sherry

2 tbsp oyster sauce

1 tbsp lime juice

1 fresh red chile, seeded and
    chopped finely

method

1 To make the dressing, place the sesame oil, fish sauce, sherry, oyster sauce, lime juice, and chile in a bowl and whisk to combine.

2 Place the mushrooms in a bowl, then cover with boiling water and let stand for 20 minutes. Drain and cut into thin slices.

3 Charbroil the beef for 5 minutes, turning once, either on a ridged grill pan or under the broiler. Cook a little longer you do not like your meat rare.

4 Slice the steak into thin strips and place in a bowl with the mushrooms, bell pepper, and nuts. Add the dressing and toss together.

5 Arrange the lettuce on a serving platter and place the beef mixture on top. Garnish with mint and serve at room temperature.

rare beef pasta salad

ingredients

SERVES 4

1 lb/450 g sirloin or top round
    steak in a single piece
4 cups small pasta, such as
    fusilli
4 tbsp olive oil
2 tbsp lime juice
2 tbsp Thai fish sauce
2 tsp honey
4 scallions, sliced
1 cucumber, peeled and cut
    into 1-inch/2.5-cm chunks
3 tomatoes, cut into wedges
1 tbsp fresh mint, finely
    chopped
salt and pepper

method

1 Season the steak with salt and pepper. Broil or pan-fry it for 4 minutes on each side. Let rest for 5 minutes, then slice thinly across the grain.

2 Meanwhile, bring a large pan of lightly salted water to a boil. Add the pasta, bring back to a boil, and cook for 8–10 minutes, or until tender but still firm to the bite. Drain the pasta, refresh in cold water, and drain again thoroughly. Toss the pasta in the olive oil and set aside until required.

3 Combine the lime juice, fish sauce, and honey in a small pan and cook over medium heat for 2 minutes.

4 Add the scallions, cucumber, tomatoes, and mint to the pan, then add the steak and mix well. Season to taste with salt.

5 Transfer the pasta to a large, warm serving dish and top with the steak and salad mixture. Serve just warm or let cool completely.

beef & peanut salad

ingredients

SERVES 4

1/2 head napa cabbage

1 large carrot

4 oz/115 g radishes

3 1/2 oz/100 g baby corn

1 tbsp peanut oil

1 red chile pepper, seeded
    and finely chopped

1 garlic clove, finely chopped

12 oz/350 g lean beef (such
    as tenderloin, sirloin, or
    top round), trimmed of
    any visible fat and sliced

1 tbsp dark soy sauce

1/4 cup fresh peanuts, optional

red chile pepper, finely sliced,
    to garnish

dressing

1 tbsp smooth peanut butter

1 tsp superfine sugar

2 tbsp light soy sauce

1 tbsp sherry vinegar

salt and pepper

method

1 Finely shred the napa cabbage and arrange attractively on a platter.

2 Peel the carrot and cut into very thin strips. Wash, trim, and quarter the radishes, and halve the baby corn lengthwise. Arrange these ingredients around the edge of the dish and set aside.

3 Heat the peanut oil in a nonstick wok or large skillet until smoking.

4 Add the red chile pepper, garlic, and beef to the wok or skillet and cook for 5 minutes.

5 Add the dark soy sauce and cook for an additional 1–2 minutes, until tender and cooked through.

6 Meanwhile, make the dressing. Place all of the ingredients in a small bowl and blend them together until smooth.

7 Place the hot cooked beef in the center of the salad ingredients. Spoon over the dressing and sprinkle with a few peanuts, if using. Garnish with slices of red chile pepper and serve immediately.

fish & seafood salads

Shellfish has always been a popular salad ingredient—crab and shrimp salads have almost become a cliché, although a very pleasant one. Some varieties of fish, such as fresh or smoked salmon and fresh or canned tuna, are also favorite ingredients, and there are others that, although less familiar in salads, are just as tasty. Perhaps this is because the delicate flavor and light texture of fish and shellfish combine so well with all kinds of salad ingredients, from pasta to fruit and from beans to arugula.

Fish and shellfish salads probably offer more scope for variety than any other type because they respond so delightfully to different flavors. Shrimp, for example, are as delicious with the Mediterranean flavors of olive oil, lemon juice, olives, and tomatoes as they are with the Southeast Asian taste of chiles and tropical fruit. Fresh vegetables and earthy lentils both complement the richness of tuna in very different but equally delicious ways. And, of course, fish and shellfish look and taste superb served together in a mixed seafood salad with a fragrant dressing.

Salads are a good way to encourage the family to eat more fish because the flavor, aroma, and texture are different from and more subtle than those of hot fish dishes, which can put some people off. They are also often very colorful, making them especially tempting.

salmon & avocado salad

ingredients

SERVES 4

1 lb/450 g new potatoes
4 salmon steaks, about
   4 oz/115 g each
1 avocado
juice of $1/2$ lemon
$1^1/_4$ cups baby spinach leaves
$4^1/_2$ oz/125 g mixed small
   salad greens, including
   watercress
12 cherry tomatoes, halved
scant $1/2$ cup chopped
   walnuts

dressing

3 tbsp unsweetened clear
   apple juice
1 tsp balsamic vinegar
pepper

method

1 Cut the new potatoes into bite-size pieces, put into a pan, and cover with cold water. Bring to a boil, then reduce the heat, cover, and let simmer for 10–15 minutes, or until just tender. Drain and keep warm.

2 Meanwhile, preheat the broiler to medium. Cook the salmon steaks under the preheated broiler for 10–15 minutes, depending on the thickness of the steaks, turning halfway through cooking. Remove from the broiler and keep warm.

3 While the potatoes and salmon are cooking, cut the avocado in half, remove and discard the pit, and peel the flesh. Cut the avocado flesh into slices and coat in the lemon juice to prevent it from discoloring.

4 Toss the spinach leaves and mixed salad greens together in a large serving bowl until combined. Divide between 4 serving plates and arrange 6 cherry tomato halves on each plate of salad.

5 Remove and discard the skin and any bones from the salmon. Flake the salmon and divide among the plates along with the potatoes. Sprinkle the walnuts over the salads.

6 To make the dressing, mix the apple juice and vinegar together in a small bowl or pitcher and season well with pepper. Drizzle over the salads and serve at once.

smoked salmon, asparagus & avocado salad

ingredients

SERVES 4

7 oz/200 g fresh asparagus
   spears
1 large ripe avocado
1 tbsp lemon juice
large handful fresh arugula
   leaves
8 oz/225 g smoked salmon
   slices
1 red onion, finely sliced
1 tbsp fresh flat-leaf parsley,
   chopped
1 tbsp fresh chives, chopped

dressing

1 garlic clove, chopped
4 tbsp extra virgin olive oil
2 tbsp white wine vinegar
1 tbsp lemon juice
pinch of sugar
1 tsp mustard

method

1 Bring a large pan of salted water to a boil. Add the asparagus and cook for 4 minutes, then drain. Refresh under cold running water and drain again. Set aside to cool.

2 To make the dressing, combine all the ingredients in a small bowl and stir together well.

3 Cut the avocado in half lengthwise, then remove and discard the pit and skin. Cut the flesh into bite-size pieces and coat in the lemon juice to prevent it from discoloring.

4 To assemble the salad, divide the arugula between 4 serving plates and top with the asparagus and avocado. Cut the smoked salmon into strips and scatter over the top of each salad, then scatter over the onion and herbs. Drizzle the dressing over the salads and serve.

tomato, salmon & shrimp salad

ingredients

SERVES 4

4 oz/115 g cherry tomatoes

several lettuce leaves

4 large ripe tomatoes,
    coarsely chopped

3$\frac{1}{2}$ oz/100 g smoked salmon

7 oz/200 g large cooked
    shrimp, thawed if frozen

dressing

1 tbsp Dijon mustard

2 tsp superfine sugar

2 tsp red wine vinegar

2 tbsp olive oil

few fresh dill sprigs, plus
    extra to garnish

pepper

method

1 Halve most of the cherry tomatoes. Place the lettuce leaves around the edge of a shallow bowl and add all the tomatoes and cherry tomatoes. Using scissors, snip the smoked salmon into strips and sprinkle over the tomatoes, then add the shrimp.

2 To make the dressing, mix the mustard, sugar, vinegar, and oil together in a small bowl, then tear most of the dill sprigs into it. Mix well and pour over the salad. Toss well to coat the salad with the dressing. Snip the remaining dill over the top and season to taste with pepper.

tuna & herby fusilli salad

ingredients

SERVES 4

7 oz/200 g dried fusilli pasta

1 red bell pepper, seeded and
quartered

1 red onion, sliced

4 tomatoes, sliced

7 oz/200 g canned tuna in
brine, drained and flaked

dressing

6 tbsp basil-flavored oil or
extra virgin olive oil

3 tbsp white wine vinegar

1 tbsp lime juice

1 tsp mustard

1 tsp honey

4 tbsp chopped fresh basil,
plus extra sprigs to garnish

method

1 Bring a large pan of lightly salted water to a boil. Add the pasta, return to a boil, and cook for 8–10 minutes, until tender but still firm to the bite.

2 Meanwhile, put the bell pepper quarters under a preheated hot broiler and cook for 10–12 minutes, until the skins begin to blacken. Transfer to a plastic bag, seal, and set aside.

3 Remove the pasta from the heat, drain, and set aside to cool. Remove the bell pepper quarters from the bag and peel off the skins. Slice the bell pepper into strips.

4 To make the dressing, put all the dressing ingredients in a large bowl and stir together well. Add the pasta, bell pepper strips, onion, tomatoes, and tuna. Toss together gently, then divide between 4 serving bowls. Garnish with basil sprigs and serve.

tuna & fresh vegetable salad

ingredients

SERVES 4

12 cherry tomatoes, halved

1¹/₂ cups whole green beans, cut into 1-inch/2.5-cm pieces

8 oz/225 g zucchini, thinly sliced

3¹/₄ cups white mushrooms, thinly sliced

generous bunch salad greens

12 oz/350 g canned tuna in brine, drained and flaked

fresh parsley, to garnish

dressing

4 tbsp mayonnaise

4 tbsp plain yogurt

2 tbsp white wine vinegar

salt and pepper

method

1 To make the dressing, put the mayonnaise, yogurt, vinegar, and salt and pepper to taste in a screw-topped jar and shake together until the ingredients are well blended.

2 Put the tomatoes, beans, zucchini, and mushrooms in a bowl. Pour over the dressing and marinate for about 1 hour.

3 Arrange the salad leaves on a serving dish. Add the vegetables and then the tuna, and garnish with parsley.

lentil & tuna salad

ingredients

SERVES 4

2 ripe tomatoes

1 small red onion

14 oz/400 g canned lentils, drained

6$^{1}/_{2}$ oz/185 g canned tuna, drained

2 tbsp chopped fresh cilantro

pepper

dressing

3 tbsp virgin olive oil

1 tbsp lemon juice

1 tsp whole-grain mustard

1 garlic clove, crushed

$^{1}/_{2}$ tsp ground cumin

$^{1}/_{2}$ tsp ground coriander

method

1 Using a sharp knife, seed the tomatoes and then chop them into fine dice. Finely chop the red onion.

2 To make the dressing, whisk together the virgin olive oil, lemon juice, mustard, garlic, cumin, and ground coriander in a small bowl until thoroughly combined. Set aside until required.

3 Mix together the chopped onion, diced tomatoes, and drained lentils in a large bowl.

4 Flake the tuna with a fork and stir it into the onion, tomato, and lentil mixture. Stir in the chopped fresh cilantro and mix well.

5 Pour the dressing over the lentil and tuna salad and season with pepper to taste. Serve immediately.

tuna & two-bean salad

ingredients

SERVES 4

7 oz/200 g green beans

14 oz/400 g canned small
white beans, such as
cannellini, rinsed and
drained

4 scallions, finely chopped

2 fresh tuna steaks, about
8 oz/225 g each and
3/4 inch/2 cm thick

olive oil, for brushing

9 oz/250 g cherry tomatoes,
halved

lettuce leaves

salt and pepper

fresh mint and parsley sprigs,
to garnish

dressing

handful of fresh mint leaves,
shredded

handful of fresh parsley
leaves, chopped

1 garlic clove, crushed

4 tbsp extra virgin olive oil

1 tbsp red wine vinegar

salt and pepper

method

1 First, make the dressing. Put the mint leaves, parsley leaves, garlic, olive oil, and vinegar into a screw-top jar, add salt and pepper to taste, and shake until blended. Pour into a large bowl and set aside.

2 Bring a pan of lightly salted water to a boil. Add the green beans and cook for 3 minutes. Add the white beans and cook for another 4 minutes, until the green beans are tender-crisp and the white beans are heated through. Drain well and add to the bowl with the dressing and scallions. Toss together.

3 To cook the tuna, heat a ridged, stove-top grill pan over high heat. Lightly brush the tuna steaks with oil, then season to taste with salt and pepper. Cook the steaks for 2 minutes, then turn over and cook on the other side for an additional 2 minutes for rare or up to 4 minutes for well done.

4 Remove the tuna from the grill pan and let rest for 2 minutes, or alternatively let stand until completely cool. When ready to serve, add the tomatoes to the bean mixture and toss lightly. Line a serving platter with lettuce leaves and pile on the bean salad. Place the tuna over the top. Serve warm or at room temperature, garnished with the herbs.

sweet & sour fish salad

ingredients

SERVES 4

8 oz/225 g trout fillets

8 oz/225 g white fish fillets
(such as haddock or cod)

1 1/4 cups water

1 stem lemongrass

2 lime leaves

1 large red chile

1 bunch scallions, trimmed
and shredded

3/4 cup diced fresh pineapple
flesh

1 small red bell pepper,
seeded and diced

1 bunch watercress, washed
and trimmed

fresh snipped chives,
to garnish

dressing

1 tbsp sunflower oil

1 tbsp rice wine vinegar

pinch of chili powder

1 tsp clear honey

salt and pepper

method

1 Rinse the fish, place in a skillet, and pour over the water. Bend the lemongrass in half to bruise it and add to the skillet with the lime leaves. Prick the chile with a fork and add to the pan. Bring to a boil and simmer for 7–8 minutes. Let cool.

2 Drain the fish fillet thoroughly, then flake the flesh away from the skin and place it in a bowl. Gently stir in the scallions, pineapple, and bell pepper.

3 Arrange the washed watercress on 4 serving plates and spoon the cooked fish mixture on top.

4 To make the dressing, mix all the ingredients together, seasoning well. Spoon it over the fish and serve the salad garnished with chives.

smoked trout with pears

ingredients

SERVES 4

1¼ cups watercress or
   arugula

1 head of radicchio, torn into
   pieces

4 smoked trout fillets, skinned

2 ripe pears, such as Bartlett

2 tbsp lemon juice

2 tbsp extra virgin olive oil

3 tbsp sour cream

2 tsp creamed horseradish

salt and pepper

thinly sliced whole-wheat
   bread, buttered, to serve

method

1 Place the watercress and radicchio in a bowl. Cut the trout fillets into thin strips and add to the bowl. Halve and core the pears, then slice thinly. Place in a separate bowl, add 4 teaspoons of the lemon juice, and toss to coat. Add the pears to the salad.

2 To make the dressing, mix the remaining lemon juice and the olive oil together in a bowl, then season to taste with salt and pepper. Pour the dressing over the salad and toss well. Transfer to a large salad bowl.

3 Mix the sour cream and horseradish together in a separate bowl until thoroughly blended and pour into a small serving bowl. Serve the salad with buttered whole-wheat bread.

skate & spinach salad

ingredients

SERVES 4

1 lb 9 oz/700 g skate wings,
　　trimmed
2 fresh rosemary sprigs
1 fresh bay leaf
1 tbsp black peppercorns
1 lemon, quartered
1 lb/450 g baby spinach
　　leaves
1 tbsp olive oil
1 small red onion, thinly sliced
2 garlic cloves, crushed
$1/2$ tsp chile flakes
$1/2$ cup pine nuts, lightly
　　toasted
$1/3$ cup raisins
1 tbsp light molasses sugar
2 tbsp chopped fresh parsley

method

1 Put the skate into a large saucepan with the herbs, peppercorns, and lemon. Cover with water and bring to a boil. Cover and simmer for 4–5 minutes, until the flesh begins to come away from the cartilage. Remove from the heat and set aside for 15 minutes. Lift the fish from the water and remove the flesh in shreds.

2 Meanwhile, put the spinach into a saucepan with just enough water to cling to the leaves. Cook over high heat for 30 seconds until wilted. Drain, refresh under cold water, and drain again. Squeeze out any excess water and set aside.

3 Heat the oil in a large skillet. Cook the onion for 3–4 minutes, until softened but not browned. Add the garlic, chile flakes, pine nuts, raisins, and sugar. Cook for 1–2 minutes, then add the spinach and toss for 1 minute, until heated through. Gently fold in the skate and cook for another minute. Season well.

4 Divide the salad among 4 serving plates and sprinkle with the parsley.

anchovies with celery & arugula

ingredients

SERVES 4

2 celery stalks, strings
    removed
4 small handfuls of arugula
12–16 brine-cured anchovy
    fillets, halved lengthwise
1¹/₂ tbsp extra virgin olive oil
salt and pepper
thick lemon wedges, to serve

method

1 Quarter the celery stalks lengthwise and slice into 3-inch/7.5-cm sticks. Soak in ice-cold water for 30 minutes, until crisp and slightly curled, then drain and pat dry.

2 Place a small pile of arugula on individual serving plates. Arrange the celery and anchovy fillets attractively on top. Spoon over a little olive oil and season with salt and pepper, bearing in mind the saltiness of the anchovies. Serve with thick wedges of lemon.

anchovy & olive salad

ingredients

SERVES 4

large handful of mixed lettuce
leaves
12 cherry tomatoes, halved
20 black olives, pitted and
halved
6 canned anchovy fillets,
drained and sliced
1 tbsp chopped fresh oregano
wedges of lemon, to garnish
crusty bread rolls, to serve

dressing

4 tbsp extra virgin olive oil
1 tbsp white wine vinegar
1 tbsp lemon juice
1 tbsp chopped fresh flat-leaf
parsley
salt and pepper

method

1 Prepare all the salad ingredients as per ingredients list. To make the dressing, put all the ingredients into a small bowl, seasoning with salt and pepper to taste, and stir together well.

2 To assemble the salad, arrange the lettuce leaves in a serving dish. Scatter the cherry tomatoes on top, followed by the olives, anchovies, and oregano. Drizzle over the dressing.

3 Transfer to individual plates, garnish with lemon wedges, and serve with crusty bread rolls.

celeriac rémoulade with crab

ingredients

SERVES 4

1 lb/450 g celeriac, peeled
and grated
juice of 1 lemon
9 oz/250 g fresh white
crabmeat, picked over
chopped fresh dill or parsley,
to garnish

rémoulade dressing

²/₃ cup mayonnaise
1 tbsp Dijon mustard
1¹/₂ tsp white wine vinegar
2 tbsp capers in brine,
well rinsed
salt and white pepper

method

1 To make the dressing, put the mayonnaise in a bowl. Beat in the mustard, vinegar, and capers, with salt and white pepper to taste— the mixture should be piquant with a strong mustard flavor. Cover and chill until required.

2 Bring a large pan of salted water to a rapid boil. Meanwhile, peel the celeriac and cut it into quarters, then grate it either in a food processor or on the coarse side of a box grater.

3 Add the grated celeriac and the lemon juice to the water and blanch for 1¹/₂–2 minutes, until it is just slightly tender. Rinse the celeriac well, then put it under cold running water to stop the cooking. Use your hands to squeeze out the excess moisture, then pat the celeriac dry with paper towels or a clean kitchen towel.

4 Stir the celeriac into the dressing, along with the crabmeat. Taste and adjust the seasoning, if necessary. Cover and chill for at least 30 minutes.

5 When ready to serve, spoon into bowls and sprinkle with dill or parsley.

cantaloupe & crab salad

ingredients

SERVES 4

12 oz/350 g fresh crabmeat

$^1/_4$ cup mayonnaise

2 fl oz/50 ml natural yogurt

4 tsp extra virgin olive oil

4 tsp lime juice

1 scallion, finely chopped

4 tsp finely chopped fresh
    parsley

pinch of cayenne pepper

1 cantaloupe melon

2 radicchio heads, separated
    into leaves

fresh parsley sprigs,
    to garnish

crusty bread, to serve

method

1 Place the crabmeat in a large bowl and pick over it very carefully to remove any remaining shell or cartilage, but try not to break up the meat.

2 Put the mayonnaise, yogurt, olive oil, lime juice, scallion, chopped fresh parsley, and cayenne pepper into a separate bowl and mix until thoroughly blended. Fold in the crabmeat.

3 Cut the melon in half and remove and discard the seeds. Slice into wedges, then cut off the rind with a sharp knife.

4 Arrange the melon slices and radicchio leaves on 4 large serving plates, then arrange the crabmeat mixture on top. Garnish with a few sprigs of fresh parsley and serve with fresh crusty bread.

chilled shrimp with pineapple & papaya salsa

ingredients

SERVES 8

4 tbsp sunflower oil

1 fresh red chile, seeded and
    chopped

1 garlic clove, crushed

48 shrimp

chopped fresh parsley,
    to garnish

pineapple & papaya salsa

1 large papaya, halved,
    seeded, peeled, and cut
    into $1/4$-inch/5-mm dice

1 small pineapple, halved,
    cored, peeled, and cut
    into $1/4$-inch/5-mm dice

2 scallions, very finely chopped

1 fresh red chile, or to taste,
    seeded and finely chopped

1 garlic clove, very finely
    chopped

$2^1/2$ tsp lemon juice

$1/2$ tsp ground cumin

$1/4$ tsp salt

black pepper

method

1 To make the salsa, put the papaya in a large bowl with the pineapple, scallions, chile, garlic, lemon juice, cumin, salt, and pepper. Adjust the lemon juice, cumin, salt, or pepper to taste, if necessary. Cover and chill until required, ideally at least 2 hours.

2 Heat a wok over a high heat. Add the oil and swirl around, then add the chile and garlic and stir-fry for 20 seconds. Add the shrimp and stir-fry for 2–3 minutes, until the shrimp are cooked through, become pink, and curl.

3 Tip the shrimp, garlic, and any oil left in the wok into a heatproof bowl and let the shrimp cool and marinate in the chile oil. When the shrimp are completely cool, cover the bowl and chill for at least 2 hours.

4 When ready to serve, give the salsa a stir and adjust the seasoning, if necessary. Arrange a mound of salsa on each of 8 plates. Remove the shrimp from the marinade and divide among plates. Sprinkle with parsley and serve.

shrimp & rice salad

ingredients

SERVES 4

scant 1 cup mixed long-grain
 and wild rice
12 oz/350 g cooked, shelled
 shrimp
1 mango, peeled, seeded,
 and diced
4 scallions, sliced
1/4 cup slivered almonds
1 tbsp finely chopped fresh
 mint

dressing

1 tbsp extra virgin olive oil
2 tsp lime juice
1 garlic clove, crushed
1 tsp honey
salt and pepper

method

1 Cook the rice in a large pan of lightly salted boiling water for 35 minutes, or until tender. Drain and transfer to a large bowl, then add the shrimp.

2 To make the dressing, mix all the ingredients together in a large measuring cup, seasoning to taste with the salt and pepper, and whisk well until thoroughly blended. Pour the dressing over the rice and shrimp mixture and let cool.

3 Add the mango, scallions, almonds, and mint to the salad and season to taste with pepper. Stir thoroughly, transfer to a large serving dish, and serve.

chile squid with watercress & baby spinach salad

ingredients

SERVES 4

12 squid tubes and tentacles
(about 1 lb 9 oz/700 g
total weight), cleaned and
prepared
2–3 tbsp olive oil
1–2 red chiles, seeded and
thinly sliced
2 scallions, finely chopped
lemon wedges, for squeezing
and for serving
3 good handfuls watercress
2 handfuls baby spinach or
arugula
salt and pepper

dressing

scant $^1/_2$ cup olive oil
juice of 1 lime
1 tsp superfine sugar
2 shallots, thinly sliced
1 tomato, peeled, seeded,
and finely chopped
1 garlic clove, crushed

method

1 To make the dressing, mix all the ingredients together in a bowl, season with salt and pepper to taste, then cover and refrigerate until required.

2 Cut the squid tubes into 2-inch/5-cm pieces, then score diamond patterns lightly across the flesh with the tip of a sharp knife. Heat the oil in a wok or large skillet over high heat, then add the squid pieces and tentacles and stir-fry for 1 minute. Add the chiles and scallions and stir-fry for an additional minute. Season to taste with salt and pepper and add a good squeeze of lemon juice.

3 Mix the watercress and spinach together, then toss with enough of the dressing to coat lightly. Serve immediately with the squid, together with lemon wedges to squeeze over the squid.

coconut shrimp with cucumber salad

ingredients

SERVES 4

1 cup brown basmati rice

$1/2$ tsp coriander seeds

2 egg whites, lightly beaten

generous $3/4$ cup dry
unsweetened coconut

24 raw jumbo shrimp, shelled

$1/2$ cucumber

4 scallions, thinly sliced
lengthwise

1 tsp sesame oil

1 tbsp finely chopped fresh
cilantro

method

1 Bring a large pan of water to a boil, add the rice, and cook for 25 minutes, or until tender. Drain and keep in a strainer covered with a clean dish towel to absorb the steam.

2 Meanwhile, soak 8 wooden skewers in cold water for 30 minutes, then drain. Crush the coriander seeds in a mortar with a pestle. Heat a nonstick skillet over medium heat, add the crushed coriander seeds, and cook, turning, until they start to color. Tip onto a plate and set aside.

3 Put the egg whites into a shallow bowl and the coconut into a separate bowl. Roll each shrimp first in the egg whites, then in the coconut. Thread onto a skewer. Repeat so that each skewer is threaded with 3 coated shrimp.

4 Preheat the broiler to high. Using a potato peeler, peel long strips from the cucumber to create ribbons, put into a strainer to drain, then toss with the scallions and oil in a bowl, and set aside.

5 Cook the shrimp under the preheated broiler for 3–4 minutes on each side, or until slightly browned.

6 Meanwhile, mix the rice with the toasted coriander seeds and fresh cilantro and divide this and the cucumber salad among bowls. Serve with the hot shrimp skewers.

shrimp & mango salad

ingredients

SERVES 4

2 mangoes (reserve the juice
   for the dressing)
2 cups peeled, cooked shrimp
salad greens, to serve
4 whole cooked shrimp,
   to garnish

dressing

6 tbsp plain yogurt
2 tbsp mayonnaise
1 tbsp lemon juice
salt and pepper

method

1 Cutting close to the pit, cut a large slice from one side of each mango, then cut another slice from the opposite side. Without breaking the skin, cut the flesh in the segments into squares, then push the skin inside out to expose the cubes, and cut away from the skin. Use a sharp knife to peel the remaining center section and cut the flesh away from the pit into cubes. Reserve any juice in a bowl and put the mango flesh in a separate bowl.

2 Add the shrimp to the mango flesh. Add the yogurt, mayonnaise, lemon juice, salt, and pepper to the juice and blend together.

3 Arrange the salad greens on a serving dish and add the mango flesh and shrimp. Pour the dressing over them and serve garnished with the whole shrimp.

ceviche

ingredients

SERVES 4

8 fresh scallops

16 large shrimp in shells

2 sea bass fillets, about
5 1/2 oz/150 g each, skinned

1 large lemon

1 lime

1 red onion, thinly sliced

1/2 fresh red chile, seeded
and finely chopped

2–4 tbsp extra virgin olive oil

to serve

salad greens

lemon or lime wedges

pepper

method

1 If the scallops are in shells, use an oyster knife or small knife to pry the shells open, then rinse under running cold water. Cut the scallops and coral free from the shells. Slice the scallop flesh into 2–3 horizontal slices each. Place in a nonmetallic bowl with the corals.

2 Remove the heads and peel the shrimp. Using a small sharp knife, devein them. Add to the scallops.

3 Cut the sea bass fillet into thin slices across the grain and add to the bowl of seafood.

4 Firmly roll the lemon and lime backward and forward on a counter to help release the juice. Cut the lemon in half and squeeze the juice over the fish. Repeat with the lime.

5 Gently stir to coat the seafood well in the citrus juices, then cover with plastic wrap, and chill in the refrigerator for 2 hours, or until the seafood becomes opaque, but do not let stand for longer otherwise the seafood will be too soft.

6 Using a slotted spoon, transfer the seafood to another bowl. Add the onion, chile, and olive oil and stir gently. Set aside at room temperature for about 5 minutes.

7 Spoon the seafood onto individual serving plates and serve immediately with salad greens, lemon or lime wedges, and black pepper.

mixed seafood salad

ingredients

SERVES 4–6

2 garlic cloves, crushed

juice of 1$\frac{1}{2}$ lemons

4 tbsp extra virgin olive oil

2 tbsp chopped fresh flat-leaf
parsley

1 lb 5 oz/600 g cooked
seafood cocktail (shrimp,
mussels, clams, calamari
rings, cockles)

1 oil-cured roasted red bell
pepper, sliced into thin
strips

12 black olives, pitted

2 tbsp shredded fresh basil

salt and pepper

method

1 Whisk the garlic, lemon juice, olive oil, and parsley with salt and pepper to taste.

2 Drain the seafood if necessary, and place in a serving dish. Add the bell pepper and olives, then mix with the garlic mixture, turning to coat. Let stand in a cool place for 30 minutes to allow the flavors to develop.

3 Stir again before serving, check the seasoning, and sprinkle with the basil.

seafood & spinach salad

ingredients

SERVES 4

1 lb 2 oz/500 g live mussels,
  soaked and cleaned
3$^1/_2$ oz/100 g shrimp, peeled
  and deveined
12 oz/350 g scallops
1 lb 2 oz/500 g baby spinach
  leaves
3 scallions, trimmed and
  sliced

dressing

4 tbsp extra virgin olive oil
2 tbsp white wine vinegar
1 tbsp lemon juice
1 tsp finely grated lemon zest
1 garlic clove, chopped
1 tbsp grated fresh ginger
1 small red chile, seeded and
  diced
1 tbsp chopped fresh cilantro
salt and pepper

method

1 Put the mussels into a large pan with a little water, bring to a boil, and cook over high heat for 4 minutes. Drain and reserve the liquid. Discard any mussels that remain closed. Return the reserved liquid to the pan and bring to a boil. Add the shrimp and scallops and cook for 3 minutes. Drain. Remove the mussels from their shells. Rinse the mussels, shrimp, and scallops in cold water, drain, and put them in a large bowl. Cool, cover with plastic wrap, and chill for 45 minutes.

2 Meanwhile, rinse the baby spinach leaves and transfer them to a pan with 4 tablespoons of water. Cook over high heat for 1 minute, transfer to a strainer, refresh under cold running water, and drain.

3 To make the dressing, put all the ingredients into a small bowl and mix.

4 Arrange the spinach on serving dishes, then scatter over half of the scallions. Top with the mussels, shrimp, and scallops, then scatter over the remaining scallions. Drizzle over the dressing and serve.

mussel salad

ingredients

SERVES 4

2 red bell peppers, halved
    and seeded
12 oz/350 g cooked, shucked
    mussels, thawed if frozen
1 head radicchio
3/4 cup arugula
8 cooked green-lipped
    mussels in their shells

dressing

1 tbsp olive oil
1 tbsp lemon juice
1 tsp finely grated lemon peel
2 tsp honey
1 tsp French mustard
1 tbsp snipped fresh chives
salt and pepper

method

1 Put the bell peppers, skin-side up, on a broiler rack and cook under a preheated broiler for 8–10 minutes, or until the skin is charred and blistered and the flesh is soft. Remove from the broiler with tongs, put into a bowl, and cover with plastic wrap. Set aside for 10 minutes, or until cool enough to handle, then peel off the skins.

2 Slice the bell pepper flesh into thin strips and put into a bowl. Gently stir in the shucked mussels.

3 To make the dressing, whisk the oil, lemon juice and peel, honey, mustard, and chives together until well blended. Season to taste with salt and pepper. Add the bell pepper and mussel mixture and toss until coated.

4 Remove the central core of the radicchio and shred the leaves. Put into a serving bowl with the arugula and toss together.

5 Pile the mussel mixture into the center of the leaves and arrange the green-lipped mussels in their shells around the edge of the bowl.

octopus with lemon & chile dressing

ingredients

SERVES 4

4 lb 8 oz/2 kg octopus,
    cleaned and gutted
1¹/₂–2 cups olive oil
juice and finely grated rind of
    1 lemon
1–2 green chiles, seeded and
    finely chopped
1–2 garlic cloves, finely
    chopped
1 tbsp chopped fresh cilantro
salt and pepper
salad greens, to serve

method

1 Preheat the oven to 350°F/150°C.

2 Place the octopus in a lidded casserole just large enough to hold it and pour in just enough olive oil to cover. Cover and cook in the preheated oven for 2 hours, until very tender.

3 Drain the octopus well and discard the cooking oil. Separate the tentacles and run your hand firmly along each one to remove the suckers. Thinly slice the tentacles and place in a bowl.

4 Mix together ¹/₂ cup of the remaining olive oil, the lemon juice and rind, chiles, garlic, and cilantro in a pitcher. Season to taste with salt and pepper and pour the dressing over the octopus. Toss gently, then cover with plastic wrap and chill in the refrigerator for at least 2 hours. Serve on a bed of salad greens.

dressings, oil & vinegars

Salad dressings are not a last-minute afterthought but an essential part of the whole dish. Freshly made dressings are always tastier than any bottle you can buy at the supermarket and you can adjust the proportions and—important from the health point of view—the amount of salt—to suit you. You will be aware from the recipes in the previous chapters that dressings are intended to complement and enhance the flavors of the salad ingredients not to smother and overpower them, and no single dressing will be satisfactory for every kind of salad. However, there are some, such as flavored vinaigrettes, that work well with many different salads and these form a useful addition to your repertoire.

An easy and delightful way of enhancing salad dressings and giving them a personal touch is to use flavored oils and vinegars. You can pay a lot of money if you buy these in the supermarket or delicatessen but they are actually astonishingly easy and economical to make at home and will keep well in a cool, dark place. Herb oils can be used for cooking as well as salad dressings, and spiced vinegars add a real gourmet touch to many meals.

tomato dressing

ingredients

SERVES 2–4

2 tbsp balsamic vinegar, or
   red or white wine vinegar
4–6 tbsp extra virgin olive oil
1 tsp Dijon mustard
pinch of superfine sugar
1 tbsp torn fresh basil leaves
1 tbsp chopped sun-dried
   tomatoes
salt and pepper

method

1 Place all the ingredients in a screw-top jar, secure the top, and shake well. Alternatively, beat all the ingredients together in a small bowl. Use as much oil as you like.

2 If you only have salad leaves to dress, 4 tablespoons of oil will be sufficient, but if you have heavier ingredients, such as potatoes, you will need about 6 tablespoons of oil.

3 Use the dressing immediately. If you want to store it, do not add the herbs—it will then keep for 3–4 days in the refrigerator.

sweet & sour dressing

ingredients

SERVES 2-4

2 tbsp lemon juice, or red or
    white wine vinegar
4–6 tbsp extra virgin olive oil
1 tsp Dijon mustard
pinch of superfine sugar
1 tbsp honey
1 tsp finely grated fresh ginger
1 tbsp toasted sesame seeds
1 tbsp freshly chopped parsley
salt and pepper

method

1 Place all the ingredients in a screw-top jar, secure the top, and shake well. Alternatively, beat all the ingredients together in a small bowl.

2 A dressing for salad leaves will require 4 tablespoons of oil, but heavier ingredients, such as potatoes, will require about 6 tablespoons of oil.

green dressing

ingredients

SERVES 4

1¹/₄ cups plain yogurt

2 tsp Dijon mustard

2–3 tbsp white wine vinegar

4 tsp sunflower oil

2 tbsp coarsely chopped
fresh parsley

2 tbsp snipped fresh chives

2 tbsp coarsely chopped
fresh tarragon

1 scallion, coarsely chopped

1 tbsp coarsely chopped
watercress

salt and pepper

method

1 Put the yogurt, mustard, vinegar, and oil into a food processor and season with salt and pepper to taste. Process on medium speed until thoroughly combined. Add the parsley, chives, tarragon, scallion, and watercress and process for a few seconds to chop finely and blend.

slim-line dressing

ingredients

1^1/$_4$ cups low-fat plain yogurt

1 tsp English mustard

2–3 tbsp lemon juice

4 tsp sunflower oil

salt and pepper

method

1 Put all the ingredients into a food processor, season with salt and pepper to taste, and process on medium speed until thoroughly combined.

garlic vinaigrette

ingredients

SERVES 2–4

$1/2$ cup garlic-flavored olive oil

3 tbsp white wine vinegar or
  lemon juice

1–2 garlic cloves, crushed

1 tsp Dijon mustard

$1/2$ tsp superfine sugar

salt and pepper

method

1 Put all the ingredients in a screw-top jar, secure the lid, and shake vigorously until an emulsion forms. Taste and adjust the seasoning if necessary.

2 Use at once or store in an airtight container in the refrigerator for up to a month. Remove the garlic cloves after 1 week. Always whisk or shake the dressing before using.

herb vinaigrette

ingredients

SERVES 2–4

1/2 cup olive or other
   vegetable oil

3 tbsp white wine vinegar or
   lemon juice

1 1/2 tbsp chopped fresh
   herbs, such as chives,
   parsley, or mint

1 tsp Dijon mustard

1/2 tsp superfine sugar

salt and pepper

method

1 Put all the ingredients in a screw-top jar, secure the lid, and shake vigorously until a thick emulsion forms. Taste and adjust the seasoning if necessary.

2 Use immediately or store in an airtight container in the refrigerator for up to 3 days. Always whisk or shake the dressing before using, and strain through a fine nonmetallic strainer if the herbs begin to darken.

basil oil

ingredients

SERVES 2–4

2 cups fresh basil leaves

2 cloves garlic, halved

1 cup olive oil

method

1 Wash the basil leaves and dry them well. Prepare a bowl of ice water.

2 Bring a saucepan of water to a boil, add the basil leaves, and blanch for five seconds. Scoop out the leaves and plunge immediately into the ice water to stop the cooking process. Drain out all the water and squeeze the leaves to get rid of as much of the water as possible. Dry them between layers of paper towels. Chop coarsely and place in a clean jar. Add the garlic.

3 Gently heat the oil over low heat until warmed and fragrant—about five minutes. Be sure that it does not boil or burn. Remove from the heat and pour the oil into a clean jar over the basil leaves. Let cool, cover, and store in the refrigerator. Strain out the basil within a week.

roasted tomato oil

ingredients

SERVES 2–4

4–6 plum tomatoes

1 cup canola oil

method

1 Preheat the oven to 400°F/200°C.

2 Thinly slice the tomatoes and place them on a lightly greased baking sheet. Place in the oven and roast until they start to char. Remove from the oven and let cool.

3 Heat the oil in a saucepan. Bring to nearly boiling and let it simmer for one to two minutes.

4 Combine the tomatoes with the warmed oil, and process in a blender or food processor. Process until the tomatoes are well incorporated into the oil. Strain through cheesecloth and pour into a clean jar. Refrigerate.

rosemary, lemon & thyme oil

ingredients

SERVES 2–4

5 sprigs rosemary (each about
   5 inches/12.5 cm long)
10–15 sprigs thyme (each
   about 5 inches/12.5 cm
   long)
zest of 2 lemons
1 cup canola oil

method

1 Preheat the oven to 300°F/150°C.

2 Remove the leaves from the rosemary and thyme sprigs. Cut the lemon zest into strips.

3 Pour the oil into a two-cup ovenproof glass measuring cup and add the leaves and lemon zest strips. Place the cup on a pie plate in the center of the oven and heat for 1^1/2–2 hours.

4 If you have a digital thermometer, test the oil. It should reach a temperature of 250°F/120°C before you remove it from the oven. Let cool for at least 30 minutes.

5 Store in the refrigerator as is, or strain through cheesecloth and refrigerate.

parsley & cilantro oil

ingredients

SERVES 2–4

$1/2$ cup fresh parsley leaves

$1/2$ cup fresh cilantro leaves

1 cup canola oil

method

1 Wash and drain the leaves. Bring a saucepan of water to a boil, and submerge the leaves. Blanch for five seconds. Drain the leaves and dry well.

2 Heat the oil in a saucepan, bring to nearly boiling and let simmer for one to two minutes.

3 Combine the warmed oil and leaves in a blender bowl or food processor. Process until well combined.

4 Pour through cheesecloth and strain into a clean jar. Cover and refrigerate.

dill & peppercorn vinegar

ingredients

SERVES 2–4

6 sprigs fresh dill

1 cup cider vinegar

1 tsp whole black
     peppercorns

method

1 Wash and dry the dill.

2 In a saucepan over medium heat, bring the vinegar to a boil. Lower the heat and simmer for 2 minutes. Add the dill and peppercorns, turn off the heat, and let sit for several minutes, until cooled.

3 Pour into a clean jar, seal, and keep in a dark place until ready to use or refrigerate.

lemongrass, ginger & garlic vinegar

ingredients

SERVES 2–4

2 stalks lemongrass
3 cloves garlic, peeled
1 tbsp grated ginger
1 cup rice wine vinegar

method

1 Wash and dry the lower portion of the lemongrass stalks, then crush or bruise them slightly. Cut them if you would like smaller pieces in the jar. Cut the garlic cloves in half lengthwise.

2 Place the lemongrass, garlic, and ginger pieces into a clean jar.

3 In a saucepan over medium heat, heat the rice wine vinegar until it starts to bubble around the edges of the pan. Remove from the heat, let cool a bit, then add to the jar with the other ingredients. When completely cool, cover the jar and store in a dark, dry place.

rosemary & garlic balsamic vinegar

ingredients

SERVES 2–4

10 sprigs of rosemary,
    2 inches/5cm long

4 cloves garlic

1 cup balsamic vinegar

method

1 Wash the rosemary sprigs, dry, and tear off the leaves from the stems. Split the garlic cloves in half lengthwise. Combine the leaves and garlic halves in a clean jar.

2 In a saucepan over medium heat, heat the balsamic vinegar until it just starts to bubble around the edges of the pan. Wait until it cools a little, then pour into the jar with the rosemary and garlic. When it is completely cool, cover the jar and store in a cool, dark place. Check occasionally to see whether the vinegar has reached the desired strength.

3 Before using, strain the vinegar through a fine strainer or cheesecloth into clean jars. Add a fresh sprig of rosemary for decoration, cover again, and store in a cool, dark place.